D0810538

PRESENTED TO

_____

BY

_____

DATE

_____

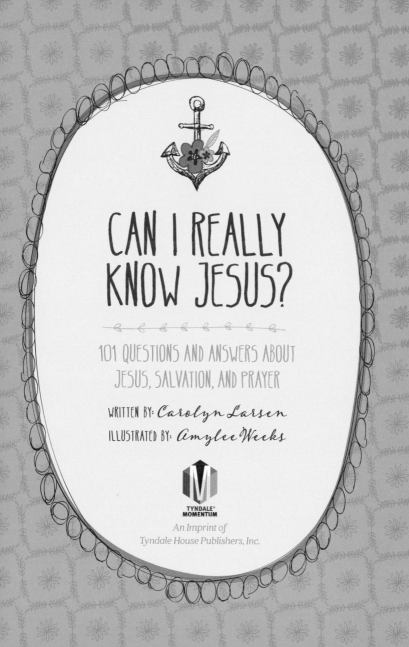

CAN I REALLY KNOW JESUS?

101 QUESTIONS AND ANSWERS ABOUT
JESUS, SALVATION, AND PRAYER

WRITTEN BY: *Carolyn Larsen*

ILLUSTRATED BY: *Amylee Weeks*

TYNDALE MOMENTUM

*An Imprint of
Tyndale House Publishers, Inc.*

Visit Tyndale online at www.tyndale.com.

Visit the author's website at www.carolynlarsen.com.

Visit the illustrator's website at www.amyleeweeks.com.

Tyndale Momentum and the Tyndale Momentum logo are registered trademarks of Tyndale House Publishers, Inc. Tyndale Momentum is an imprint of Tyndale House Publishers, Carol Stream, Illinois.

Can I Really Know Jesus?: 101 Questions and Answers about Jesus, Salvation, and Prayer

Designed by Jennifer Ghionzoli

Published in association with Educational Publishing Concepts, PO Box 655, Wheaton, IL 60187.

ISBN 978-1-4964-1175-4

Printed in China

22   21   20   19   18   17   16
7   6   5   4   3   2   1

INTRODUCTION

FAITH IS BELIEF OR CONFIDENCE in something, even when the object of faith cannot be fully grasped in the physical realm. A relationship with God is based on faith in him. It's a growth process of learning to accept and appreciate his grace, mercy, and love. The "instruction manual" God has given us—the Bible—helps us understand who God is and shows us how to live for him, obey him, trust him, and love him. But even with this source of amazing help and the commitment to engage in life with God through faith, we sometimes have questions.

Questions aren't wrong. In fact, they're helpful because they express a desire to learn and understand. However, it's important to search for answers to your questions from a reliable source that is true to Scripture. _Can I Really Know Jesus?_ answers 101 frequently asked questions that are common to those who are investigating faith in Jesus Christ.

Some questions are about Jesus and why he came, how he lived, and what he taught. Others explore God's wonderful plan of salvation, made possible by Jesus' sacrificial death on the cross. And some are about the great privilege and mystery of prayer—communicating with God. It is our hope that this book will help answer some of your questions and pave the way to a strong faith in God.

ACKNOWLEDGMENTS

○ ○ ○ ○ ○ ● ○ ○ ○ ○ ● ○ ○ ○

Writing a book like this one carries with it the responsibility to be true to Scripture, to not mislead readers, and to honor and revere God. It is not something that can be accomplished alone. So I wish to thank the wonderful people at Tyndale House Publishers for their wisdom, input, and support. I appreciate Tyndale's standard of excellence and desire to honor God in every book they publish. Thank you, Anisa Baker and Becky Brandvik, for your vision for this book. Thank you to Anne Christian Buchanan for your attention to detail and "big picture" plan. It's been a privilege to work with all of you.

Carolyn Larsen

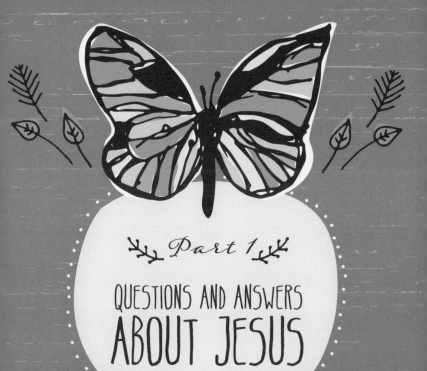

Part 1

QUESTIONS AND ANSWERS ABOUT JESUS

Q. CAN I REALLY KNOW JESUS?

I hear a lot of talk about Jesus, but who is he exactly?

A. The Bible states clearly that Jesus is the Son of God. In fact, he is God, one of the three "persons" of God—the Father, Son, and Holy Spirit—that together are called the Trinity. Jesus was present from the very beginning of time. But a little more than two thousand years ago, God the Father called on Jesus to come to earth as a human—the culmination of God's plan to rescue the world from the grip of sin.

On earth, Jesus taught about God and how to live. He also performed many miracles. But some political and religious leaders of the time were jealous of him, so he was arrested, condemned, and brutally executed on a cross.

But that's not the end of the story! God raised Jesus back to life, breaking the power of sin and death in the world. You see, when Jesus died on the cross, he was taking upon himself the punishment that really belonged to us sinful humans. God offers forgiveness and eternal life to those who confess their sins and accept what Jesus did for them. They are given a new heart and enter into a relationship with him that is personal, like having a close friend. Yes, you can really know Jesus—and live with him forever !

All who declare that Jesus is the Son of God have God living in them, and they live in God.   1 JOHN 4:15

Q. HOW CAN WE KNOW JESUS REALLY EXISTED?

Was he an actual historical person or just a myth or legend?

A. The Bible, of course, tells us that Jesus existed as a human on earth. But there is also evidence from other respected sources that Jesus was a real historical person.

One of those sources was a Jewish historian named Josephus, who lived in the first century and wrote a history of the Jews from Adam to the time of the Roman emperor Nero. He mentioned Jesus three different times.

The Roman historian Tacitus, writing at about the same time, also mentioned Jesus, his crucifixion, and Nero's persecution of Christians. Tacitus's friend Pliny the Younger, a governor in Asia Minor, sent letters to the Roman emperor Trajan describing Pliny's treatment of early Christians. Neither of these Romans were Christian believers. They just reported what they had seen and heard.

Some people interpret comments in the Talmud, a compilation of Jewish doctrine, as coded references to Jesus and his followers, providing further evidence that Jesus existed.

○ ○ ○ ○ ○ ○ ○ ● ○ ○ ○ ● ○ ● ○ ○ ○ ○ ○ ● ○ ○ ○ ● ○ ○ ○ ● ○ ○

[Paul] explained and testified about the Kingdom of God and tried to persuade them about Jesus from the Scriptures. . . . Some were persuaded by the things he said, but others did not believe. ACTS 28:23-24

Q. WHY IS JESUS CALLED "CHRIST"?

Is "Christ" his last name?

A. While "Jesus" is the name the angel Gabriel told Mary to give her baby, "Christ" is a title—not a last name—that shows his position as the one God chose to deliver his people.

The word *Christ* comes from the Greek word *Christos*, the Greek equivalent of the Hebrew word *Mahshiach*, which is translated as *Messiah* in English. Both words mean "anointed one" or "chosen one."

When kings came into power in Bible times, they were anointed with olive oil mixed with spices as a way of dedicating them to God's service. Calling Jesus the "anointed one" shows his position and power. He is the anointed one who fulfills Old Testament prophecies foretelling the coming of a chosen one—the Messiah—who would deliver the Israelites from oppression. So using the name Christ for Jesus is the same as saying that he is the chosen one.

- -

The Spirit of the LORD is upon me, for he has anointed me to bring Good News to the poor. He has sent me to proclaim that captives will be released, that the blind will see, that the oppressed will be set free. LUKE 4:18

Q. IS JESUS THE "SON OF GOD" OR THE "SON OF MAN"?

He couldn't be both at the same time, could he?

A. Jesus is called the "Son of God" because he came from God the Father. But he also often called himself the "Son of Man." Matthew 8:20 and John 13:31 are just a few examples.

Jesus was born of a woman—Mary—so he is the "Son of Man." But in becoming human, Jesus did not stop being God. He only left his place in heaven to live among the people he had created and to serve as an example of how they should live.

The people of Jesus' day would have been familiar with the title "Son of Man" since the prophet Daniel used the term when he was clearly referring to the promised Messiah: "I saw someone like a son of man coming with the clouds of heaven. . . . He was given authority, honor, and sovereignty over all the nations of the world. . . . His rule is eternal—it will never end. His kingdom will never be destroyed" (Daniel 7:13-14).

So when Jesus called himself the "Son of Man," he was confirming his humanity but also signaling to his listeners his role as the Messianic judge, deliverer, savior, and vindicator described in the book of Daniel.

- -

The high priest asked him, "Are you the Messiah?" . . . Jesus said, "I AM. And you will see the Son of Man . . . coming on the clouds of heaven. MARK 14:61-62

Q. WHY IS JESUS CALLED "THE WORD"?

I thought the Bible was the Word of God.

A. The first chapter of the Gospel of John paints a beautiful picture of who Jesus is and how he came to earth to bring light to our darkness. But that beautiful passage doesn't refer to him as "Jesus." Instead, it calls him "the Word." Why?

Basically, "the Word" is a biblical term for God's communication with human beings. The Bible *is* the Word of God, but Jesus is a form of God's communication too—in fact, the most important form. By sending his Son to earth, God was telling people that he loved them, that despite their sin he hadn't given up on them, and that he was willing to do whatever it took to rescue the human race from its dark and fallen existence.

In Jesus, God was showing us himself—the best form of communication of all.

In the beginning the Word already existed. The Word was with God, and the Word was God. . . . And his life brought light to everyone. The light shines in the darkness, and the darkness can never extinguish it. JOHN 1:1, 4-5

Q. WHAT IS "THE INCARNATION"?

And what does it have to do with Jesus?

A. The term *incarnation* is very important because it gets to the heart of what Jesus did for us. This word literally means "the act of becoming flesh" and refers to a spiritual being taking on human form. That's what Jesus did when he was born and grew up to be a man. He ate and drank, walked and talked, taught others, and worked with his hands. He had parents, siblings, and friends. He knew what it felt like to be hungry, thirsty, lonely, and tempted—and eventually to suffer and die.

But Jesus was no ordinary man. Although fully human, he was also fully God. That double identity makes a huge difference. Because he lived as a human, Jesus understands our struggles. And because he is God, he lived a perfect human life without sin. When he died on the cross to take the penalty for our sins, he also conquered death. Jesus' incarnation was a true game changer for the entire human race.

The Word became human and made his home among us. He was full of unfailing love and faithfulness. And we have seen his glory, the glory of the Father's one and only Son. JOHN 1:14

Q. IS JESUS MENTIONED IN THE OLD TESTAMENT?

Did people know Jesus was coming? Does the Old Testament say anything about him?

A. The people of Jesus' day did not know specifically that the coming Messiah would be named Jesus, but they did have Scriptures—now part of our Old Testament—that foretell the coming of a Savior, an anointed one called the Messiah.

Isaiah 7:14 says the Messiah would be born from a virgin and would be called Immanuel, which means "God is with us." Isaiah 9:6-7 speaks about his birth and the power and influence he would have. This passage also predicts he would be called by names like "Mighty God" and "Prince of Peace." Isaiah 53 prophesies the Messiah's suffering and death for our sins. And Micah 5:2 mentions the Messiah would be born in Bethlehem.

All of these prophecies were fulfilled in the life of Jesus. But many who eagerly awaited the Messiah were surprised by what he did and said. They were expecting a political leader who would lead them to independence from the Roman government. Instead, they encountered God in human flesh, who, true to prophecy, died to save them from their sins.

∘ ∘

A child is born to us, a son is given to us. The government will rest on his shoulders. And he will be called: Wonderful Counselor, Mighty God, Everlasting Father, Prince of Peace. ISAIAH 9:6

Q. DID JESUS KNOW WHAT WAS GOING TO HAPPEN TO HIM WHEN HE CAME TO EARTH?

Did he actually agree to come knowing that he would have to go through suffering?

A. It's hard to believe that someone would voluntarily go into a situation involving great pain and even death—through no fault of his or her own. But Jesus did that. He came knowing he would suffer and die for the sins of others. He also knew that first he would spend time teaching people about God and performing many miracles. He knew that some people would believe in him—and that others would not.

These people, including religious and political leaders of Jesus' day, looked for ways to turn against him. When they arrested him, he knew what was ahead—torturous beatings and a brutal death. Jesus could have called angels to rescue him, but he didn't.

He willingly went through it all because of his love for the people he had created . . . his love for you.

○ ○ ● ○ ○ ○ ○ ● ● ○ ○ ○ ○ ○ ○ ○ ○ ○ ● ○ ○ ○ ○ ○

Jesus fully realized all that was going to happen to him, so he stepped forward to meet them. "Who are you looking for?" he asked. JOHN 18:4

Q. IS CHRISTMAS DAY REALLY JESUS' BIRTHDAY?

Is December 25 the actual day he was born? How can we know?

A. No one knows for certain the date of Jesus' birth, but it is unlikely that December 25 is truly his birthday. Some Bible scholars believe he was more likely born in either spring or fall because the Bible says that shepherds were out in the fields watching their sheep the night he was born. If he had been born in winter, the sheep would have been kept in pens at night. We also know that the town of Bethlehem, where Jesus was born, was crowded with people who had returned for the Roman census. It is unlikely that such an event would take place in the winter, when traveling was difficult.

People began celebrating December 25 as Jesus' birthday some three hundred years after Jesus returned to heaven. They may have chosen that date because other festivals were already being observed then. Even if Christmas is not the actual date of his birth, it's a wonderful time to celebrate Jesus as God's gift to humankind!

While they were there, the time came for her baby to be born. She gave birth to her firstborn son. She wrapped him snugly in strips of cloth and laid him in a manger, because there was no lodging available for them. LUKE 2:6-7

Q. WHY DID GOD CHOOSE MARY TO BRING JESUS INTO THE WORLD?

Was there something special about her?

A. Mary was just an ordinary young woman when the angel Gabriel came to tell her that she was going to have a special baby. But the Bible says that she had found favor with God, so she must have been serious about knowing God and living for him.

It was also important that Mary was not married. She was a virgin, so there was no doubt that God was Jesus' father. Her unmarried state allowed her to fulfill Isaiah's prophecy that the Messiah would be born of a virgin (Isaiah 7:14).

It must have been scary for Mary when the angel appeared and told her she was going to be the mother of Jesus. But Mary was devoted to serving God, so she was willing to do whatever God wanted her to do.

Mary responded, "I am the Lord's servant. May everything you have said about me come true." And then the angel left her. LUKE 1:38

Q. WHY DID SOMEONE TRY TO KILL JESUS WHEN HE WAS A BABY?

Why would anyone want to harm an innocent child?

A. It all started when a group of men from eastern lands stopped in Jerusalem. They were following a star in the sky; to them, it indicated a very special king had been born. Herod was the king of Judea at that time, and when he heard the men were looking for this "newborn king of the Jews" (Matthew 2:2), he wasn't about to take chances with a possible rival for his throne. Knowing that Old Testament prophecies stated the Messiah would be born in Bethlehem, the jealous king ordered all boys in that area who were under the age of two to be murdered. This terrible event had also been foretold in the Old Testament.

God protected Jesus, though. In a dream, an angel told Joseph, Mary's husband, to immediately take Jesus and Mary to Egypt. So they escaped that night and didn't return until Herod had died.

∘ ○ ∘ ○ ∘ ○ ○ ∘ ○ ∘ ○ ● ○ ∘ ○ ∘ ○ ○ ○ ○ ○ ● ○ ∘ ○ ● ○ ○

A cry was heard in Ramah—weeping and great mourning. Rachel weeps for her children, refusing to be comforted, for they are dead. MATTHEW 2:18

Q. WHAT DO WE KNOW ABOUT JESUS' EARLY LIFE?

What was he like as a boy?

A. The Bible doesn't tell us much about Jesus' childhood; however, there's one story of a time when he was twelve years old and had traveled to Jerusalem with his parents for the Passover feast. When it was time for them to return home, Jesus stayed behind in Jerusalem. The Bible says that Jesus' parents assumed he was walking with others—a hint that he had friends to spend time with. But by evening, they discovered that Jesus wasn't with the other travelers. Mary and Joseph returned to search for him. Three days later, they found him at the Temple. He was asking questions and listening to the teachers, who were very impressed with his knowledge. After his parents found him there, he obediently went home with them.

Since the Bible doesn't tell us anything else about Jesus' life until he was thirty years old, it's likely that he had a normal childhood for a boy of that time—playing with friends, completing schoolwork, studying God's Word, and doing household chores. His earthly father, Joseph, was a carpenter, so Jesus probably helped him in his work.

○ ○ ○ ○ ○ ○ ○ ○ ○ ○ ○ ● ● ● ● ○ ○ ○ ○ ○ ○ ○ ● ○ ○ ○ ● ○ ○

Jesus grew in wisdom and in stature and in favor with God and all the people. LUKE 2:52

Q. DID JESUS HAVE BROTHERS OR SISTERS?

Did Mary have more children after Jesus was born?

A. Some people have not wanted to believe that Mary had other children, but there are references in the Gospels to Jesus' brothers and sisters. They would have actually been his half brothers and half sisters because Mary conceived Jesus by the Holy Spirit and her other children by her husband, Joseph. Jesus' four half brothers are mentioned by name in Matthew 13. There is also a reference to sisters, but they are not named, and we do not know how many there were.

According to the Bible, some of Jesus' family members and neighbors had a hard time understanding who he was. At one point after he began his traveling ministry around age thirty, his brothers ridiculed him (John 7:5). Another time, his family objected to Jesus and his disciples not having time to even eat and tried to take him away from the crowd that had gathered (Mark 3:20-21). Eventually, though, at least some of Jesus' brothers believed he was the Messiah. And it is likely that Mary had always understood his messianic role.

- -

They scoffed, "He's just the carpenter's son, and we know Mary, his mother, and his brothers—James, Joseph, Simon, and Judas. All his sisters live right here among us. Where did he learn all these things?" MATTHEW 13:55-56

14

Q. WHO WAS JOHN THE BAPTIST?

And why was he called "Baptist" anyway?

A. John was related to Jesus. How? He was the son of Mary's cousin Elizabeth—and he understood who Jesus really was. John spent his time in the wilderness and lived off the land, dressing in clothes made of camels' hair and eating locusts and wild honey. He had a ministry of helping people face their sins and baptizing them as a sign of repentance. *Baptism* is a translation of the Hebrew term for immersion in water. This ritual was an Israelite tradition that signified spiritual cleansing, and that's why John is called "the Baptist."

John dedicated his life to preparing people to meet Jesus. His ministry of announcing that Jesus was coming was foretold in the Old Testament—Isaiah prophesied that a lone voice in the wilderness would announce the Messiah was coming. This was the focus of John's ministry. It got people thinking about how they had fallen short of God's standards and their need for change since someone even greater was coming soon. That person was Jesus, the Messiah.

John told them, "I baptize with water, but right here in the crowd is someone you do not recognize. Though his ministry follows mine, I'm not even worthy to be his slave and untie the straps of his sandal." JOHN 1:26-27

Q. WHY WAS JESUS BAPTIZED?

Jesus hadn't ever sinned, so why did he ask John to baptize him?

A. John was baptizing people in the Jordan River, where they dipped into the water to symbolize they had turned away from their sins and wanted to live new lives. Then Jesus showed up and wanted to be baptized. John was reluctant: He knew who Jesus was—that Jesus had no sin to turn away from. But Jesus insisted. Why would he do that?

Jesus' baptism is significant for a few reasons. For one, it fulfilled the Old Testament prophecies about the Messiah— the Holy Spirit came and rested upon him as a dove (Isaiah 11:2), and with an audible voice, God the Father spoke his approval over Jesus (Psalm 2:7). For another, it showed that he identified with people who were considered righteous because they recognized their need to stop sinning.

John's form of baptism—where people lowered themselves into the water and came back up—is a beautiful symbol of Jesus' death and resurrection. Being baptized is an act of obedience to God's way. In his baptism, Jesus displayed humility as he anticipated his ministry to repentant people.

❧ ❧ ❧ ❧ ❧ ❧ ❧ ❧ ❧ ❧ ❧ ❧ ❧ ❧ ❧

After his baptism, as Jesus came up out of the water, the heavens were opened and he saw the Spirit of God descending like a dove and settling on him. And a voice from heaven said, "This is my dearly loved Son, who brings me great joy." MATTHEW 3:16-17

Q. WHICH RELIGION DID JESUS FOLLOW?

Or did he make up his own religion since he is God?

A. Jesus did not make up a religion. He followed a faith that was already established—Judaism. Growing up in a Jewish family, Jesus attended synagogue, visited the Temple, observed Jewish holy days like Passover, and studied the Hebrew Scriptures.

Though Jesus was faithful to his Jewish upbringing, he did interpret and clarify Old Testament Scripture in fresh new ways, helping people understand what God really wanted from his people. And when Jesus died on the cross, came back to life in his resurrected body, and later ascended to heaven, he laid the foundation of a new kind of faith that would be open to all people, not just his fellow Jews.

Jesus said to the people who believed in him, "You are truly my disciples if you remain faithful to my teachings. And you will know the truth, and the truth will set you free." JOHN 8:31-32

Q. DOES JESUS UNDERSTAND TEMPTATION?

How could he if he is God?

A. If you had nothing to eat for forty days and nights, you'd be pretty hungry and weak. Would you find it hard to resist temptation if enticing things were offered to you? When Jesus went out into the wilderness to pray, he was faced with this very situation, yet he did not give in (see Matthew 4).

Jesus had eaten nothing for forty days when Satan said, "Why don't you turn these stones into bread?" Hungry as he was, Jesus quoted Scripture instead: "People do not live by bread alone, but by every word that comes from the mouth of God." Satan then took Jesus to the highest point of the Temple in Jerusalem and said, "If you are the Son of God, jump off! For the Scriptures say, 'He will order his angels to protect you.'" But Jesus again said no: "You must not test the LORD your God." After that, Satan took him to the top of a high mountain and showed him the kingdoms of the world, saying, "I will give it all to you . . . if you will kneel down and worship me." Jesus replied in no uncertain terms: "Get out of here, Satan. . . . The Scriptures say, 'You must worship the LORD your God and serve only him.'"

○ ○ ○ ○ ○ ○ ○ ○ ○ ○ ● ● ○ ○ ● ○ ○ ○ ○ ○ ○ ○ ○ ● ○ ○ ○ ○ ○ ○

This High Priest of ours understands our weaknesses, for he faced all of the same testings we do, yet he did not sin.

HEBREWS 4:15

Q. COULD JESUS HAVE SINNED?

Was it even possible for him to disobey God?

A. The Bible says specifically that Jesus *did not* sin—not even after those forty days of fasting in the wilderness and being tempted by Satan. But *could* he sin?

Jesus was fully human, which means that theoretically he could have chosen to sin. He had a body and a brain, so he experienced physical, mental, and emotional urges that would have at times tempted him to do the wrong thing. But remember, Jesus was also fully God, so Jesus' divine nature gave him the power to resist temptation and choose not to sin.

None of this is spelled out in the Bible, and many people find it hard to wrap their minds around the paradox. But two things should be clear: (1) Jesus understands your temptation to sin because he experienced it firsthand, and (2) Jesus did not give in to temptation, and he will help you fight your own.

∘ ∘

Keep watch and pray, so that you will not give in to temptation. For the spirit is willing, but the body is weak! MATTHEW 26:41

Q. WHO WERE JESUS' FIRST FOLLOWERS?

Were they men who held important positions in society?

A. Jesus' public ministry began after his temptation experience in the wilderness. He chose twelve men as his inner circle of disciples, and he would have several other followers as well, including women who supported him financially (see Luke 8:1-3).

The first disciples Jesus chose were brothers: Simon (later called Peter) and Andrew. They were fishermen until Jesus called them to leave their nets and follow him. Next came another pair of brothers: James and John. Soon after that, Philip, Bartholomew (also called Nathanael), Thomas, Matthew (a tax collector), another James (called James, son of Alphaeus), Thaddeus, another Simon (called Simon the Zealot), and Judas Iscariot rounded out the list of Jesus' first twelve followers.

Jesus' disciples were ordinary men who left their lives behind to follow him. They shared his life and traveling ministry. When Jesus went back to heaven, he left them with the responsibility of sharing the truth of his love and forgiveness with others.

[Jesus told his disciples,] "You will receive power when the Holy Spirit comes upon you. And you will be my witnesses, telling people about me everywhere—in Jerusalem, throughout Judea, in Samaria, and to the ends of the earth." ACTS 1:8

Q. WHAT WAS JESUS' FIRST MIRACLE?

Did he do any miracles when he was a child?

A. As far as we know, Jesus didn't do any miracles when he was a boy. The Bible says he performed his first miracle around age thirty, after he had been baptized and had chosen his disciples. Shortly after that the disciples went with Jesus and his mother to a wedding in the town of Cana.

Apparently he did not plan to do a miracle that day. When the wedding hosts ran out of wine and Jesus' mother asked him to help, he said that his time for performing miracles had not yet come. Mary, who evidently had great faith in her eldest son, ignored him and told the servants to do whatever he told them. So Jesus obliged his mother and asked them to fill six jars with water and draw some out for the master of ceremonies to taste. The water had changed to wine—better wine than the hosts had originally served.

Jesus' disciples had followed him because they thought he was someone special. When they saw the miracle, they truly believed that he was.

This miraculous sign at Cana in Galilee was the first time Jesus revealed his glory. And his disciples believed in him. JOHN 2:11

Q. WHAT LANGUAGE DID JESUS SPEAK?

Did he speak in Hebrew—the same language that the Old Testament was written in?

A. Yes and no. Most experts agree that Jesus spoke Aramaic on an everyday basis. It was the common language of the Jewish people at the time he lived. He was probably familiar with Hebrew because the Scriptures, written in Hebrew text, were read in the synagogues. Jesus himself read a portion from Isaiah at his boyhood synagogue in Nazareth.

Jesus may have spoken some Greek as well since it was considered the international language of the day and was often used for official or intellectual discussions. There was even a Greek translation of the Hebrew Scriptures available—the Septuagint. When Jesus was arrested and brought before the Roman governor of Judea, Pontius Pilate, he may have responded to questions in Greek.

Of course Jesus could have spoken any language he wanted to, but it's a reasonable guess that he chose to speak the languages that the people around him would understand.

∘ ∘

The people were amazed at his teaching, for he taught with real authority—quite unlike the teachers of religious law. MARK 1:22

Q. IF JESUS IS GOD, WHY DID HE PRAY *TO* GOD?

Isn't that sort of like talking to himself?

A. Remember that before Jesus' incarnation, he was with God, his Father, in heaven. No doubt they communicated frequently, even constantly. So when Jesus began his earthly ministry, he continued that communication by praying to his Father often. We know that Jesus experienced the challenges of living in a fallen world, as well as resistance from those who did not believe in him, so it's understandable that he asked for strength, wisdom, and power. And he was not talking to himself but staying in touch with his strength and support base. God the Father, God the Son (Jesus), and God the Holy Spirit are equally God but distinct in their roles.

Jesus' habit of frequent prayer set a good example for his followers and taught them about the necessity of staying in touch with God. It's a good reminder for us, too. If Jesus needed to stay in touch with God the Father, then we surely do also.

○ ○ ○ ○ ○ ○ ○ ○ ○ ○ ● ○ ● ○ ● ○ ○ ○ ○ ○ ○ ● ○ ○ ○ ● ○ ○

Jesus looked up to heaven and said, "Father, thank you for hearing me. You always hear me, but I said it out loud for the sake of all these people standing here, so that they will believe you sent me." JOHN 11:41-42

23

Q. WHAT WAS JESUS' MOST IMPORTANT TEACHING?

I know he taught a lot of important things, but is there something I need to learn first?

A. Jesus taught many important things about knowing God and living for him. One well-known collection of his teachings is the Sermon on the Mount, which you can read in Matthew 5–7. This amazing passage is packed with information about what it means to live a God-honoring life. But an even more concise summary of Jesus' teachings can be found in Matthew 22. When asked, "What is the most important commandment?" Jesus responded with a simple statement that boiled down all of his other teachings to two simple commands—love God and love others. He even said that all of God's law is based on these two statements. That is the place to start when it comes to following Jesus.

- -

Jesus replied, "You must love the Lord your God with all your heart, all your soul, and all your mind. This is the first and greatest commandment. A second is equally important: Love your neighbor as yourself." MATTHEW 22:37-39

Q. WHY DID JESUS TEACH LESSONS THROUGH STORIES?

Why didn't he just tell people outright what he wanted them to know?

A. Jesus was a master storyteller. But he didn't just tell stories. He told *parables*—short stories that illustrate a moral or spiritual point. He knew that people often learn better by hearing stories than by being taught rules or lessons.

Some Bible stories you might be familiar with are parables, such as the one about the Good Samaritan (Luke 10:30-37) or the Prodigal Son (Luke 15:11-32). Some parables are long, while some are very short and read more like examples than actual stories. But all of them center on objects and experiences that were familiar to the people he was teaching—fishing, sheep herding, salt, bread. When Jesus told parables, many people listened and learned the lessons he wanted them to learn.

Not everyone, though. In fact, another reason Jesus spoke in parables was that he knew they wouldn't make sense to everyone. Some people followed him just because of his miracles, not because they wanted to know God. Still others were actively trying to get him in trouble. Jesus hid his teachings from these people by putting them in parable form.

- -

He taught them by telling many stories in the form of parables. MARK 4:2

Q. DID JESUS EVER ACTUALLY SAY HE WAS GOD?

Or did he just let people figure it out?

A. There is no place in the Bible where Jesus is quoted as directly saying, "I am God." But he did say things that indicated this was true.

Even when he was just a boy and his family thought he was lost, they found him in the Temple talking with the teachers. "Didn't you know I must be in my Father's house?" he asked when his parents scolded him (Luke 2:49).

As an adult, he often said things such as, "The Father and I are one" (John 10:30), which makes it pretty clear that he and his Father are part of the same reality. They are both God.

Jesus replied, "Have I been with you all this time, Philip, and yet you still don't know who I am? Anyone who has seen me has seen the Father! So why are you asking me to show him to you?" JOHN 14:9

Q. DID JESUS REALLY WALK ON WATER?

How could he do that—and why?

A. The disciples had just seen Jesus feed more than five thousand people with only five loaves of bread and two fish. They didn't understand how he did it, and they weren't yet clear about who he was, but they saw it happen. Then Jesus told them to get in a boat and cross the Sea of Galilee while he stayed behind to pray. When the winds picked up, the disciples were stranded out on the water. They were afraid they were going to die.

Jesus came to them in the midst of the wind and waves, walking on top of the water. When he climbed into the boat, the wind stopped. How was he able to do that? He is in command of all of nature—he created it. By walking on water and calming the wind and waves, he was showing the confused disciples two things: first, that he was God, and second, that he would protect them because he cared about them. That night the disciples recognized Jesus as God's Son.

⸙ ⸙ ⸙ ⸙ ⸙ ⸙ ⸙ ⸙ ⸙ ⸙ ⸙ ⸙ ⸙

The disciples worshiped him. "You really are the Son of God!"
they exclaimed. MATTHEW 14:33

Q. HOW COULD PETER WALK ON TOP OF THE WATER TO JESUS?

Why didn't he sink?

A. When Jesus was walking on the wavy water toward the disciples, they were huddled together and terrified they were going to drown. At first they weren't sure that the figure coming toward them was Jesus—they thought it was a ghost. But Jesus reassured them it was him.

Peter called out, "Lord, if it's really you, tell me to come to you, walking on the water." Jesus answered, "Yes, come" (see Matthew 14:28-29). Peter stepped out onto the water and began walking toward Jesus. How amazing that must have felt.

What kept Peter on top of the water? He was buoyed by his trust in Jesus and his belief that Jesus had called him to come. But then Peter's trust faltered. He took his eyes off of Jesus and noticed the waves and the wind. At that moment he began to sink, and Jesus had to reach out and rescue him.

Peter's experience is a great lesson in keeping our eyes on Jesus and not on our present worries. Trust him no matter what's going on in your life. He will take care of you.

○ ○

The LORD is my strength and shield. I trust him with all my heart. He helps me, and my heart is filled with joy. I burst out in songs of thanksgiving. PSALM 28:7

Q. WHY DID JESUS SPEND SO MUCH TIME WITH SINNERS?

Why didn't he spend more time with the "good" people?

A. In a way, that's a trick question. Jesus came to save sinners, and every person Jesus encountered was a sinner.

But Jesus did spend a lot of his time with people whom society looked down on as morally corrupt or unimportant—tax collectors, prostitutes, beggars, women, and children. Why did he focus his attention on them? That answer is simple: They were open to learning about God's love. Some were sinners who knew their lives weren't working and wanted to change, and others wanted to identify with a man who gave them worth.

On the other hand, the political and religious leaders refused to acknowledge their sin. They thought they knew all the answers and did not want to learn anything from Jesus. In fact, they even considered Jesus' words and actions as blasphemous.

Wealth, education, social standing, or even a reputation for righteousness didn't matter to Jesus. His ministry was to those who wanted to know God and understood their need for him.

○ ○ ○ ○ ○ ○ ○ ○ ○ ● ● ○ ○ ○ ○ ○ ○ ○ ○ ○ ● ○ ○ ○ ○ ○ ○

Jesus . . . told them, "Healthy people don't need a doctor—sick people do. I have come to call not those who think they are righteous, but those who know they are sinners." MARK 2:17

Q. WHY DID RELIGIOUS LEADERS OF JESUS' DAY DESPISE HIM SO MUCH?

Didn't they know who he was?

A. The religious leaders of Jesus' day considered him a threat to their system and authority. They were angry about the claims he made and the way he ignored rules they thought were highly important.

Jesus' popularity was a problem for these leaders as well. They were jealous of the power he had over people. They especially hated his tendency to call out their hypocrisy, lack of love, judgmental spirits, and arrogance. And they disapproved of the people he often associated with because they were considered sinners or outcasts.

The bottom line is that the religious leaders feared Jesus and felt they had to stop him. So they lied about him to the Roman authorities, incited the crowd against him, and arranged for his arrest and a quick trial that led to his crucifixion. They thought everything would go back to normal once he was dead, but they were wrong. God brought Jesus back to life, and he is still changing lives today. His story can't be stopped!

Jesus said . . . "What sorrow awaits you teachers of religious law and you Pharisees. Hypocrites! For you shut the door of the Kingdom of Heaven in people's faces." MATTHEW 23:1, 13

Q. DID JESUS EVER GET ANGRY?

Some people were hateful toward him. Did he ever get mad in response? Or did he get angry with his followers when they didn't understand what he was telling them?

A. Jesus was remarkably patient. As far as we know, he never lost his temper when people misunderstood or mistreated him. But the Bible does relate a few times when he got angry.

On more than one occasion, Jesus told off the religious leaders who objected to what he was doing. The Gospel of Luke (13:10-17) records a time when he healed a woman on the Sabbath, and the religious leaders accused him of breaking the law because he desecrated the Sabbath day by "working." Jesus was so annoyed that he called them hypocrites to their faces.

And Jesus got *really* angry when he and his followers went to the Temple and found money changers and merchants cheating people who needed to purchase animals for sacrifices required by the law. He grew so furious that he turned over their tables and chairs and drove them away with a whip!

So yes, Jesus got angry, but not for his own sake. His anger was righteous anger, motivated by a deep love for upholding God's laws and protecting his people.

A day of anger is coming, when God's righteous judgment will be revealed. ROMANS 2:5

Q. WHY DID JUDAS BETRAY JESUS?

Judas was one of Jesus' closest friends. Why would he betray him?

A. Jesus spent three and a half years teaching his disciples about God's true nature. They witnessed multiple miracles and observed his interactions with all kinds of people. You'd think that by then they would have understood who Jesus was. Yet several disciples still didn't get it. And in exchange for money, one of them, Judas, ended up betraying Jesus to the religious authorities who wanted to stop him.

Why did Judas do this? We don't know for certain. He may have been disappointed that Jesus wasn't going to overthrow the oppressive Roman government and set up an earthly kingdom. Or perhaps he was worried Jesus would find out he'd been taking money from their common treasury. One Old Testament prophecy indicated the Messiah would be betrayed by someone close to him, and another indicated he would be betrayed for thirty pieces of silver. Judas fulfilled those Scriptures.

Even so, when Judas found out Jesus would be executed, he was sorry he had betrayed Jesus. He returned the money he'd received, but it didn't change the situation. Judas killed himself shortly afterward.

° °

Even my best friend, the one I trusted completely, the one who shared my food, has turned against me. PSALM 41:9

Q. DID JESUS REALLY SWEAT DROPS OF BLOOD IN THE GARDEN OF GETHSEMANE?

That doesn't sound real. Is it even possible?

A. The Gospel of Luke says that Jesus' sweat fell "like great drops of blood." So it's possible that's just a way of saying he perspired heavily. However, there is an extremely rare physical condition called hematidrosis that can cause a person to sweat blood. Tiny blood vessels that surround the sweat glands in the body rupture and leak blood into the sweat glands. Some experts believe this can be caused by great stress or anxiety.

We don't know if Jesus actually had hematidrosis, but we do know he was under great stress. Because he is God, he knew what was going to happen after he was arrested in the garden. And because he is human, he dreaded it. He even prayed and asked his Father to spare him but acknowledged he wanted his Father's will to be done above his own. Even though Jesus was in terrible distress, he didn't run away or try to avoid his arrest. He chose to face torture and death so that his Father's plan could be accomplished.

He prayed more fervently, and he was in such agony of spirit that his sweat fell to the ground like great drops of blood. LUKE 22:44

Q. DID JESUS FEEL PAIN WHEN HE WAS TORTURED AND KILLED?

He was human, but he was also God. So did he really feel pain?

A. After Jesus was arrested, he endured terrible torture and beatings. He was killed in an especially painful way—nailed to a cross to suffer slow suffocation. The fact that Jesus was God did not spare him from feeling the pain of these experiences.

Jesus went through terrible agony as he took the punishment for our sins. Jesus felt every lash from the whip, every beating from human hands, every laceration from the crown of thorns pressed down on his head, and every blow of the hammer on the nails. He felt it all. He was not spared from the pain, and he chose not to be. Why? Because he wanted us to know how much he loves us.

The sacrifice of Jesus was not easy, and it wasn't cheap. The Son of God, who never sinned, willingly took on our sin so that we could be saved. That's what love does.

- -

Christ suffered for our sins once for all time. He never sinned, but he died for sinners to bring you safely home to God. He suffered physical death, but he was raised to life in the Spirit. 1 PETER 3:18

34

Q. WHY DID JESUS HAVE TO DIE?

Jesus is God's Son. Couldn't he have stopped the people from crucifying him?

A. Jesus didn't *have* to die on the cross. He *chose* to—because he loves us. He wanted to make a way for each of us to know God personally.

God is perfect; he does nothing wrong. He will not allow any sin into his presence. Since all human beings are sinners, God had to make a choice—banish us forever from his presence or provide payment and cleansing for our sins so we could live in fellowship with him. Because of God's tremendous love for us, he chose the latter.

Before Jesus' day, people sacrificed animals as payment for their sins. But that stopped when Jesus became our sacrifice through his death on the cross. He took our punishment so that we can stand innocent before God and have a rich relationship with him. More than that, we have the promise of eternal life with him in heaven when our earthly lives are finished. It pleases God to give us such a tremendous gift, and we can live in peace knowing our future is in his hands.

- -

God presented Jesus as the sacrifice for sin. People are made right with God when they believe that Jesus sacrificed his life, shedding his blood. ROMANS 3:25

35

Q. DID GOD THE FATHER REALLY DESERT JESUS WHEN HE WAS DYING ON THE CROSS?

Why would he do that? Didn't he love Jesus?

A. According to Matthew 27:46, Jesus cried out these words while hanging on the cross: "My God, my God, why have you abandoned me?" But does this mean God really abandoned Jesus in his suffering and death?

This question has been debated for years. You can do research and find answers to support several viewpoints. But it's helpful to realize that when Jesus cried out, he was actually quoting Psalm 22:1, which he had probably memorized at an early age. Many people believe that Psalm 22, with its description of a jeering crowd and enemies gambling for garments, is a prophecy of Jesus' crucifixion, so his use of these words indicates he knew exactly what was going on. Even more, that psalm contains an affirmation that God *doesn't* desert those who are suffering. This can lead us to believe that, although Jesus did suffer greatly, God the Father was there the whole time, loving him through the torture and pain and standing ready to complete his plan for redeeming humankind.

Praise the LORD! . . . He has not ignored or belittled the suffering of the needy. He has not turned his back on them, but has listened to their cries for help. PSALM 22:23-24

Q. DID JESUS REALLY RISE FROM THE DEAD?

Is there any proof that the Resurrection is true?

A. Jesus lived in a prescientific age, so there is no scientific proof of his resurrection. But there is a lot of compelling evidence that it happened.

To start, there was the empty tomb and the guards who would likely face death if they fell asleep on their watch. There's the fact that no one ever found Jesus' body. There were the eyewitnesses—up to five hundred—who claimed they had seen the risen Jesus. There were the terrified, confused disciples who had suddenly become confident, fearless, and willing to die for their claim that Jesus had risen. There was Saul, a fierce persecutor of Jesus' followers, who encountered Jesus in a vision and became the famous apostle Paul. And there's the fact that a little band of persecuted believers somehow grew to be a worldwide phenomenon that has continued for two thousand years.

Are you convinced? If not, study this issue some more. Many people find the evidence not only convincing but also life changing.

If Christ has not been raised, then ... all who have died believing in Christ are lost! ... But in fact, Christ has been raised from the dead. He is the first of a great harvest of all who have died. 1 CORINTHIANS 15:17-20

Q. WHY DIDN'T JESUS' FOLLOWERS RECOGNIZE HIM AFTER HE WAS RESURRECTED?

They knew him so well. Wouldn't they instantly know him?

A. Mary Magdalene came to Jesus' tomb to put spices on his body. Upset to find him missing, she approached the "gardener" to ask him what had happened. Only when the man said her name—"Mary"— did she realize she was talking to Jesus!

A similar thing happened to some disciples who were walking on the road to Emmaus. A "stranger" joined them and struck up a conversation. The disciples invited him to dinner, but they didn't recognize the stranger as Jesus until he broke the bread.

Remember, these people were tired, confused, and very upset. And though Jesus had told them he would rise from the dead, they hadn't understood, so they weren't expecting to see him. In Mary's case, it was early in the morning and may have still been dark. And it's possible that Jesus didn't *want* to be recognized right away. Scripture says that at first God kept the disciples on the road to Emmaus from recognizing who Jesus was. But Jesus did eventually make himself known to his followers. They spoke with him and even ate with him several times before he ascended to heaven.

○ ○ ○ ○ ○ ○ ○ ○ ○ ● ○ ○ ● ○ ○ ○ ○ ○ ● ○ ○ ○ ● ○ ○ ○ ● ○

Mary Magdalene found the disciples and told them, "I have seen the Lord!" JOHN 20:18

Q. WHY DID JESUS FORGIVE PETER FOR DENYING HIM?

Wasn't he angry that his friend had abandoned him at such a critical time?

A. Jesus predicted that Peter would deny him three times—and Jesus was right. After Jesus was arrested, bystanders asked Peter three times if he was a disciple, and each time Peter denied knowing Jesus. This was the disciple whose name Jesus had changed from Simon to Peter—which means the Rock!

We don't know where Peter went after his third shameful denial. But we do know he saw Jesus after the Resurrection. This time Jesus asked Peter three times, "Do you love me?" Each time Peter said yes, Jesus responded by saying something like "Take care of those I love." He not only forgave Peter but also gave him a job to do.

Jesus forgave Peter because he knew his disciple was so very sorry for denying him. Jesus knows we will all fail him sometimes. He looks at our hearts to see if our true longing is to obey him and honor him. If so, he's always ready to give us another chance.

∘ ∘

Now I say to you that you are Peter (which means "rock"), and upon this rock I will build my church, and all the powers of hell will not conquer it. MATTHEW 16:18

Q. WHERE IS JESUS NOW?

Jesus came back to life, but what happened to him after that?

A. Just three days after Jesus died, God raised him back to life. Some time after that, he appeared to all of his disciples and to more than five hundred of his other followers. About forty days after Jesus' resurrection, Scripture tells us that he ascended—rose up in the air—and finally disappeared. His disciples watched him go. After he disappeared into the clouds, two angels spoke to them and promised that Jesus would return to earth one day in the same way he had left.

Before he died, Jesus told his followers that he was going to heaven to prepare a place for them (and for us). So that's where he is now—in heaven. Scripture tells us that he sits in a place of honor at God's right hand. But Scripture also confirms the angels' message that Jesus will come back again to usher in a new age—eventually with a "new heaven and a new earth" (Revelation 21:1).

Now Christ has gone to heaven. He is seated in the place of honor next to God, and all the angels and authorities and powers accept his authority.   1 PETER 3:22

Q. WHAT HAPPENED TO JESUS' DISCIPLES?

Did they stay close or disperse after Jesus' death?

A. After Jesus returned to heaven, his disciples did exactly what he had told them to do. All of them (except Judas, who killed himself) went out into the world to spread the Good News about Jesus, and most of them eventually paid with their lives for doing so.

Where did they go? Most of our information comes from old traditions, and some has been disputed, but it is believed that Peter was martyred in Rome and Andrew in Greece. James was executed by Herod Agrippa, son of the king who tried to kill Jesus as a baby. John wasn't martyred but was persecuted for his faith and exiled to an island called Patmos. Thomas traveled to Syria and ended up in India, where he was speared to death. We're not as sure about what happened to the other disciples, but tradition has them traveling to Africa, Persia, Asia Minor, and even the British Isles.

[Jesus said,] "Go and make disciples of all the nations, baptizing them in the name of the Father and the Son and the Holy Spirit. Teach these new disciples to obey all the commands I have given you." MATTHEW 28:19-20

Q. IS JESUS THE ONLY WAY TO GOD?

Other religions claim there are different ways to get to heaven. Is following Jesus really the only way?

A. Jesus said it himself: "I am the way, the truth, and the life. No one can come to the Father except through me" (John 14:6). God made it possible for people to personally know him by sending his Son, Jesus, to take the punishment for our sins. John 3:16 says that God sent his *only Son* so that people would believe in him and gain eternal life.

Other religions may be led by good and wise people, but God's Word makes it very clear that there is only one way to God—through Jesus. It can be confusing when you're bombarded by such a large array of different philosophies, but remember that any teaching that goes against the Bible is false teaching. So don't accept any other pathways. Follow the only one that is true: Jesus.

There is one God and one Mediator who can reconcile God and humanity—the man Christ Jesus. 1 TIMOTHY 2:5

Q. HOW CAN JESUS HELP ME TODAY?

I know I will be with him in heaven someday, but how can he help me with my everyday life?

A. There are many promises in Scripture as to what Jesus will do for you—right now, in the midst of your daily life. He will give you strength in difficult situations. He will care for you when you're hurting. He will give you wisdom when you have decisions to make. He will give you courage when you're afraid. He will help you find forgiveness when you come to him with your guilt. These are just some of the promises in Scripture.

So what do you need help with today? Jesus wants to be a part of your life. He wants to help you, strengthen you, celebrate you, guide you, love you, and give you purpose. All you have to do is ask him.

Give all your worries and cares to God, for he cares about you. 1 PETER 5:7

43

Q. WHY SHOULD I TRUST JESUS?

It's hard to trust someone I don't see face-to-face. How do I know he will take care of me?

A. Trusting Jesus is basic to the Christian life. Trusting him means that you actually dedicate your life to him by obeying him and serving him. But why should you do that? *How* can you do it?

The reason is love! Jesus loves all of us so much that he endured mockery, false accusations, and ultimately a painful death to take the punishment that we deserved. He wants to protect you, guide your decisions, and help you become the best person you can be. He wants to show you how to live for God and serve him. He will not do anything that does not move you in the right direction.

If you have any doubts about this, talk to some people who have followed Jesus for a while. They will be able to share some personal experiences of how Jesus came through for them and will help you see that Jesus is worthy of your trust.

- -

Trust in the LORD with all your heart; do not depend on your own understanding. Seek his will in all you do, and he will show you which path to take.   PROVERBS 3:5-6

44

Q. WHEN WILL JESUS COME AGAIN?

Jesus said he would return to earth, but that was a long time ago. When is he coming?

A. Over the years, many people have guessed when Jesus will return, and so far they have all been wrong. Jesus said that no one except God the Father—not even Jesus himself—knows when it will happen.

The Bible does mention some signs that indicate Jesus' return is getting close: "wars and threats of wars," earthquakes and famines, false prophets who claim to be Jesus, increasing evil in the world. Sounds familiar, doesn't it? But such signs have been appearing ever since Jesus ascended. It's sort of like when a woman is ready to give birth. The labor pains may start and stop, then start again. We know the birth will happen, but *when* is anyone's guess.

What should we do while we're waiting? The Bible is clear about this. We simply keep our heads up and live the way Jesus has shown us—by loving God with all our hearts and loving others as ourselves.

- -

No one knows the day or hour when these things will happen, not even the angels in heaven or the Son himself. Only the Father knows. And since you don't know when that time will come, be on guard! Stay alert! MARK 13:32-33

THE HEAVENS
DECLARE
THE GLORY OF GOD;
THE SKIES PROCLAIM
THE WORK
OF HIS HANDS.

PSALM 19:1, NIV

Part 2

QUESTIONS AND ANSWERS ABOUT SALVATION

45

Q. WHAT DOES IT MEAN TO "BE SAVED"?

Saved from what?

A. To understand what this means, you first need to face the fact that you're a sinner. We all are! Every human is prone to break God's laws. We can't seem to stop ourselves, even when we try. We lie. We hate. We do what we know is wrong and fail to do what we know is right. And because God is absolutely holy and perfect, he cannot coexist with sin, which means we cannot have a relationship with God or go to heaven when we die.

It's hopeless . . . or it would be, except that Jesus died to pay the penalty for each of our sins. To receive that gift, you need to feel genuine sorrow for your sins, confess them to Jesus, ask for his forgiveness, and purpose in your heart to love him. Jesus' sacrifice on the cross is what "saves" you from being condemned to life without God and the prospect of eternity in hell. Being saved also means that Jesus offers guidance, strength, and help throughout your life. Now that's a true gift!

The wages of sin is death, but the free gift of God is eternal life through Christ Jesus our Lord. ROMANS 6:23

Q. WHAT DOES IT MEAN TO "ACCEPT" JESUS?

Why do people tell me I need to "accept" Jesus? Accept him as what?

A. Think of it this way. You cannot really enjoy a gift or benefit that is offered to you until you choose to receive it. That's really what accepting Jesus means—choosing to receive the free gift that has been offered to you by his incarnation, life, death, and resurrection.

Jesus died on the cross to give us a way out of our sinfulness and to connect us with God. The gift he offers as a result—purchased at such great cost—includes forgiveness, an intimate relationship with God, and eternal life. But we cannot benefit from Jesus' sacrifice unless we accept it. That means we do our best to follow his teachings and we put our faith and trust in him as the one who saves us from sin.

If you openly declare that Jesus is Lord and believe in your heart that God raised him from the dead, you will be saved. ROMANS 10:9

Q. ISN'T IT ENOUGH JUST TO BE A GOOD PERSON?

If I am good and kind, will that be enough to help me get into heaven?

A. Being honest, thoughtful, and kind is certainly a good way to behave. It may earn you respect and help you get along well with other people. Also, it probably feels good when you show such thoughtfulness.

But is being good and kind all you need to get into heaven? No, it is not. The Bible makes it very clear that even the sum total of our good deeds cannot outweigh one transgression of God's perfect law. The only pathway to heaven is through accepting Jesus as your Lord and Savior. That's it. There is no other way. It is wonderful to be good and show kindness to others—Jesus wants that! But to get to heaven, you must surrender your life to him.

We are all infected and impure with sin. When we display our righteous deeds, they are nothing but filthy rags. ISAIAH 64:6

48

Q. WHAT DOES IT MEAN TO BE "BORN AGAIN"?

That doesn't even make sense. How can I be born again when I'm already an adult?

A. "Born again" is kind of a confusing term, but it comes straight from Jesus. When a man named Nicodemus was talking with Jesus, Jesus told him that no one can truly understand God and his Kingdom without being born again.

Jesus explained the term by saying that just as we are all born into physical life—delivered by our mothers into the world as babies—there is a spiritual birth too. It happens when we ask Jesus to be our Savior because it is then that the Holy Spirit (God's Spirit) comes to live in our hearts. The Spirit guides us and challenges us to know God and live for him.

"Born again" thus means being born into God's family through faith in Jesus. Like a baby, we still have a lot of growing and learning to do, but something fundamental in us has changed. In a sense we have become what the apostle Paul calls "a new person" (2 Corinthians 5:17).

Jesus replied, "I tell you the truth, unless you are born again, you cannot see the Kingdom of God." JOHN 3:3

Q. WHAT IS GRACE?

It's a good thing, right? What can I do to get it?

A. The word *grace* comes from a Greek word that means favor, blessing, or kindness. In the Bible this word is used over and over to describe God's basic attitude toward us. He gives us good things—including second chances—even though we don't deserve them. We don't have to earn his grace. In fact, there's no way we *can* earn it. All we can do is accept it with gratitude.

God's grace began when he continued to care for Adam and Eve instead of abandoning them because they disobeyed him. His grace continued as he kept promises to his people, gave them laws for guidance, and provided them countless chances to stop sinning and return to him. His greatest act of grace was sending Jesus to die for our forgiveness. Today he continues to show grace to those who come to him through Jesus.

Grace is God's greatest gift to those who deserve it the least. And it's available to you today, right now.

Let us come boldly to the throne of our gracious God. There we will receive his mercy, and we will find grace to help us when we need it most. HEBREWS 4:16

Q. WILL I STOP HAVING PROBLEMS AFTER I'M SAVED?

Life will be super smooth and easy after I accept Jesus, right?

A. Wouldn't that be wonderful? But no, being saved doesn't mean you'll no longer have problems. In fact, you might have a few *more* problems because Satan will do whatever he can to pull you away from God.

But here's the difference: After you're saved, you can turn to God and ask him to help you face your problems. You will learn to trust his guidance, so there will be less to worry about. And when you mess up (you will!), you can come to him for forgiveness and leave your guilt behind.

Having problems is just part of living in this world where sin still exists. God doesn't promise to take away those problems, but he does promise to be with you through all of them. He will give you strength, peace, and forgiveness.

○ ○ ○ ○ ○ ○ ○ ○ ○ ● ● ● ○ ○ ○ ○ ○ ○ ○ ○ ○ ● ○ ○ ○ ● ○ ○

Can anything ever separate us from Christ's love? Does it mean he no longer loves us if we have trouble or calamity, or are persecuted, or hungry, or destitute, or in danger, or threatened with death? . . . No, despite all these things, overwhelming victory is ours through Christ, who loved us. ROMANS 8:35, 37

51

Q. WILL I BE DIFFERENT AFTER I'M SAVED?

Will I feel different? Look different? Will people be able to tell that I accepted Jesus?

A. You probably won't look that different. But people *may* notice something different about you. They may say that you seem different because you are more peaceful or happy. That's a good thing!

When you first put your trust in Jesus, you will probably feel different. It's like you have a new best friend. You may feel giddy and joyful or more confident. If you had a lot of worries and guilt before, you might feel relieved and free. All of that is good too.

Keep in mind that those feelings may change over time. You probably won't always feel happy or relieved. But you will still be different from your old self because you will know how much Jesus loves you and have an ongoing relationship with him. You'll have his guidance and comfort, and you'll know he's always with you.

- -

My old self has been crucified with Christ. It is no longer I who live, but Christ lives in me. So I live in this earthly body by trusting in the Son of God, who loved me and gave himself for me. GALATIANS 2:20

52

Q. CAN ANYONE BE SAVED?

What about people who have done horrible things?

A. Yes, anyone can be saved. Some people have committed horrible sins—done terrible things to other people and even ended up in prison. But if they open their hearts to Jesus and ask for his forgiveness, he gives it. He pardons their sins and becomes their Savior. They are "born again," and the process of becoming a new person begins. This can happen even at the last minute of their lives. It was true for a criminal who was crucified right next to Jesus. He had committed grievous sins, but Jesus saved him when he asked.

This is hard to understand from a human viewpoint—especially if you or a loved one has been hurt by someone who has since repented and now believes in Jesus. But if you ask God to help you forgive that person, you can celebrate that God has saved them because they are truly sorry for what they have done.

- — — — — — — — — — — — — — — — — — — —

He brought them out and asked, "Sirs, what must I do to be saved?" They replied, "Believe in the Lord Jesus and you will be saved, along with everyone in your household." ACTS 16:30-31

Q. HOW DO I RECEIVE GOD'S FORGIVENESS?

All I have to do is ask? Really?

A. As amazing as it sounds, you can come to the God who created everything—the God who controls time, the God who sacrificed his only Son for you—and ask him to forgive all the wrong things you have done. When you do that, he will forgive you completely.

God's forgiveness is a wonderful gift. All you have to do to receive it is to acknowledge your sins to him, ask for his forgiveness, and sincerely ask Jesus to guide you and be in charge of your life. That's what it means to ask Jesus to be your Lord and Savior. Will you feel forgiven? Probably—he gives his peace when we come to him with sincere hearts. But even if you don't, stand in faith that because you have asked, God has forgiven you.

God longs to have a good relationship with you. He's waiting for you, so don't hesitate to go to him. He will graciously give you his forgiveness and show you his heart of love. Remember to thank him too!

He is so rich in kindness and grace that he purchased our freedom with the blood of his Son and forgave our sins. EPHESIANS 1:7

Q. DO I NEED TO ASK FOR SALVATION MORE THAN ONCE?

Sometimes I think Jesus didn't come into my heart when I asked him to. Do I need to keep asking?

A. It's dangerous to base your faith on how you are feeling at any given moment because your feelings change according to what mood you're in. If you're sad or depressed, it's more difficult to feel God's presence with you. That's when you may start to wonder whether Jesus really did come into your heart.

When you ask Jesus into your heart, he comes. You are saved, and you cannot be unsaved. You belong to Jesus for all time, and he will never let you go.

Try to stay close to God by reading his Word, praying, and living the way he wants you to live. That feeling of Jesus being far away will eventually disappear.

[Jesus said,] "My sheep listen to my voice; I know them, and they follow me. I give them eternal life, and they will never perish. No one can snatch them away from me, for my Father has given them to me, and he is more powerful than anyone else. No one can snatch them from the Father's hand." JOHN 10:27-29

Q. HOW CAN I BE SURE I'M SAVED?

I still do bad things sometimes. How do I know if I'm really saved?

A. When you ask Jesus to be your Savior, he comes into your heart and stays. That doesn't mean you will never sin again! There will be times when you disobey God's commands, when you are unkind or selfish, when you do wrong things or fail to do what's right. That's just a sad part of being human. But it doesn't mean your salvation isn't real.

The Bible says that when you invite Jesus into your heart, he *does* come in. It doesn't say that he might come or that he will only stay for a little while. Jesus loves you, and you can believe what he says. So trust in your salvation, even when you know you've messed up. Acknowledge your sin, ask God to forgive you, and start fresh, trusting that all is well between you and God. It is. And don't despair—over time, Jesus will help you grow stronger in your areas of weakness. When you are sincerely trying to follow God and his ways, you never have to doubt your salvation.

Look! I stand at the door and knock. If you hear my voice and open the door, I will come in, and we will share a meal together as friends. REVELATION 3:20

56

Q. DOES KNOWING I'M SAVED FOREVER MEAN I CAN DO ANYTHING I WANT?

Can I continue sinning and just ask Jesus to forgive me?

A. Some people may be tempted to view salvation as permission to sin. It's true that Jesus will forgive your sins when you ask him with a sincere heart, but let's look at the bigger picture.

When you ask Jesus to be your Savior, it's because you trust him and understand that he loves you very much. As you get to know him better, you develop a real relationship with him. So would you deliberately do things that grieve the heart of Jesus, even if you can later ask him to forgive you?

Of course not. When you have come to Jesus for salvation, you don't take his forgiveness for granted or treat it lightly. Instead, you try to obey him more because you love him with greater measure each day. Instead of finding an excuse to do what *you* want, you seek to do what *God* wants.

Will you slip up at times and sin? Yes. And then you'll need to acknowledge your shortcomings and freshly receive God's forgiveness. But you won't desire to use his grace as a "get out of jail free" card.

○ ○

Should we keep on sinning so that God can show us more and more of his wonderful grace? Of course not! Since we have died to sin, how can we continue to live in it? ROMANS 6:1-2

Q. WHAT IS BAPTISM?

What does it mean?

A. Baptism is something Jesus commanded before he went back to heaven. It is an outward display of the inward change in your heart.

Churches approach baptism in different ways. In some, people are lowered under the water (a picture of Jesus' death, burial, and resurrection), while in others, water is poured or sprinkled over the head of the person being baptized.

Churches also differ as to *when* a person can be baptized. All baptize adults and older children who make the decision to accept Jesus. But some also baptize infants as a sign of the parents' and the church's commitment to raise them in the Christian faith. These babies will later be "confirmed" when they are old enough to willingly decide that they will follow Jesus.

Whatever the church tradition, baptism is always done "in the name of the Father and the Son and the Holy Spirit" (Matthew 28:19), and all forms of baptism symbolize the washing away of sin and the beginning of a new life in Christ.

You were buried with Christ when you were baptized. And with him you were raised to new life because you trusted the mighty power of God, who raised Christ from the dead. COLOSSIANS 2:12

58

Q. DO I NEED TO BE BAPTIZED TO BE SAVED?

Am I not a Christian until I am baptized?

A. Baptism is an act of obedience to Jesus and a way of identifying with him. Remember, Jesus himself was baptized, even though he had no sins to repent of. However, baptism is not a requirement for salvation. Specific verses in Scripture make it clear that salvation comes by God's grace to us—it's his gift—and it is based on our faith in Jesus, not on any "things" we do. There is even an example in Scripture of a man to whom Jesus promised salvation but who did not have the chance to be baptized—the criminal who died beside him on the cross.

Choosing to be baptized after accepting Jesus as your Savior is a public display of your commitment to follow him and to be part of the community of those who love him. It is not necessary to the salvation process.

God saved you by his grace when you believed. And you can't take credit for this; it is a gift from God. Salvation is not a reward for the good things we have done, so none of us can boast about it. EPHESIANS 2:8-9

59

Q. AFTER I'M SAVED, DO I HAVE TO ASK GOD TO FORGIVE EVERY SINGLE THING I DO WRONG?

What if I forget to ask him to forgive me for something? What happens then?

A. God promises that when you invite Jesus into your heart, he forgives your sins. But he still instructs that throughout your life, you need to seek his forgiveness when you sin. Why? For one, it causes you to stop and think about the things you've done. It makes you see the areas in your life you need to work on. Second, it keeps you honest, and when there is open communication, you stay close to God.

But is it really possible to ask God to forgive every negative thought, every unkind word, every single sin? Probably not. And that's not really a problem, because when you place your faith in Jesus for salvation, all of your sins are forgiven—past, present, and future. So you don't have to remember each specific sin—just stay aware of the attitude of your heart. Jesus died to pay the penalty for all your sins, and when they are forgiven, they all are forgiven.

* * *

Repent of your sins and turn to God, so that your sins may be wiped away.   ACTS 3:19

Q. WHAT HAPPENED TO PEOPLE WHO BELIEVED IN GOD BEFORE JESUS CAME?

Jesus said that he is the only way to God, so how could people be saved if they lived before he did?

A. It is true that the focus of salvation is belief in Jesus, which directs the believer to faith in God. But there are many examples in the Old Testament of men and women whom God considered righteous because of their great faith in him. Noah, Abraham and Sarah, Moses, and David are just a few. They all knew God before Jesus lived on earth.

The best way to understand their salvation is that they believed based on the amount of information they had about God. Since Jesus' death, the news spread that Jesus was God's Son and that he purchased our redemption on the cross. He taught, suffered, died, and was resurrected so we could shed the guilt of our sins and know God in a personal way. From that time on, belief in Jesus has been the doorway to salvation. Faith in God has always been the ultimate goal, but the pathway to that faith changed when Jesus came.

○ ○ ○ ○ ○ ○ ○ ○ ○ ○ ○ ● ○ ○ ○ ○ ○ ○ ○ ○ ● ○ ○ ○ ● ○ ○

Ever since the world was created, people have seen the earth and sky. Through everything God made, they can clearly see his invisible qualities—his eternal power and divine nature. So they have no excuse for not knowing God. ROMANS 1:20

61

Q. IS THERE A SIN THAT CANNOT BE FORGIVEN?

Is there anything I can do that is so bad that God won't forgive me?

A. Jesus speaks of only one sin that cannot be forgiven—"blasphemy against the Holy Spirit" (Matthew 12:31). That means accusing God's Holy Spirit of evil things. Some of the religious leaders of Jesus' time had accused him of being demon possessed. That's what Jesus was talking about.

However, since Jesus died for our sins, it is not really possible to commit this sin to the point of it being unforgivable. People may disclaim God, ignore him, and fight against him, but if they then accept Jesus and ask for his forgiveness, they will receive it. Hearts change when they turn to God.

There is only one sin today that cannot be forgiven, and that is to not surrender to Jesus as one's Lord and Savior. God does not refuse to forgive those who humble themselves and acknowledge their need to repent and receive forgiveness. Jesus' death and resurrection make that forgiveness possible.

If we confess our sins to him, he is faithful and just to forgive us our sins and to cleanse us from all wickedness. 1 JOHN 1:9

62

Q. WHAT HAPPENS TO CHRISTIANS WHO SIN?

Aren't people supposed to stop sinning once they have accepted Jesus? Does God get mad if we keep sinning?

A. Every single person sins—no matter their status in life or how long they have been a Christian. We can try not to sin. We can pray for God's strength to keep us from sinning. But there are times when we still sin because it is in our nature to have sinful thoughts and do unkind things. Ever since Adam and Eve disobeyed God, all humans have had sin in their hearts.

The difference between how we view sin before we're saved and afterward is that as Christians, we long to stop sinning. Not only that—we now have God's Holy Spirit within us, which gives us the power of a renewed mind to increasingly overcome sinful habits and desires. It doesn't mean we'll never sin, but thankfully God knows that our desire is to obey him. So, when Christians sin and ask for God's forgiveness, we receive it because God loves us so very much.

- - - - - - - - - - - - - - - -

If we claim we have no sin, we are only fooling ourselves and not living in the truth. 1 JOHN 1:8

Q. WHAT IS "SANCTIFICATION"?

I've heard Christians use this word. What does it mean? Is it something I need to do?

A. "Sanctification" is related to the word *saint*. It means to be made holy. But *holy* doesn't mean what a lot of people think it means. It doesn't mean to be sinless or perfect. It means to be set aside for God's purposes.

Picture it this way: All the people, things, activities, and buzz of the world are standing together as a group, but you step out and move *away* from it and *toward* God. You are separated and set aside for special use—his use.

Jesus said that sanctification happens by the truth of God's Word (John 17:18-19). This happens at the moment we accept Jesus, and it continues as we grow to be more and more like Jesus. But it's not something we do for ourselves. We cannot make it happen. Sanctification is God's work accomplished by the Holy Spirit in the hearts of Christians. It is evidence that we are connected to God forever.

⤙⤙⤙⤙⤙⤙⤙⤙⤙⤙⤙⤙⤙⤙⤙⤙

God's will was for us to be made holy by the sacrifice of the body of Jesus Christ, once for all time. HEBREWS 10:10

64

Q. DOES GOD HAVE A PLAN FOR MY LIFE?

I know he wants me to be saved, but what about after that?

A. God's plan for your life is that you come to Jesus, acknowledge your need for his forgiveness and guidance, and spend the rest of your days enjoying his fellowship, serving him, telling others about who he is and what he has done for you. But does he have a more specific plan, such as what career you should choose or whom you should marry? Does he care what college you go to or who your friends are?

God does desire to lead you. In fact, he asks you to pray for his guidance and help throughout your life. He will direct your choices so you end up in the best places to serve him, learn about him, and use your talents and gifts for him. But you must be patient. God reveals things a step at a time, so keep praying and seeking his counsel. And don't worry too much about "missing" what God has in mind. Just as God forgives sins, he can redeem the missteps we make in life. If you keep on seeking him, God can use even your goofs and detours as part of his plan for your eventual good and for his glory.

"I know the plans I have for you," says the LORD. "They are plans for good and not for disaster, to give you a future and a hope." JEREMIAH 29:11

Q. AM I SUPPOSED TO TELL OTHERS ABOUT JESUS?

Isn't that the job of a minister or an evangelist?

A. There are two different destinations that await people after they die. One is heaven—eternal life with God. The other is hell—an eternity of condemnation without God's loving presence. Where a person goes depends on whether they have asked for Jesus' forgiveness and acknowledged that he is Lord of all. Once a person dies and is condemned to hell, he or she doesn't get another chance to go to heaven. So knowing about God's love and Jesus' sacrifice and not telling others is selfish. When you know about Jesus, you know the best news there is. How can you not share it with others so they can make their own choice about him?

The work of *evangelism*—sharing the Good News—is for every Christian, not just professional ministers and preachers. Maybe you can't preach a sermon or explain difficult Bible verses, but you can share what has happened in your life and say, "God cares about you. I'm praying for you." You can also model the gospel by how you live and how you show his love to others.

○ ○ ○ ○ ○ ○ ○ ○ ○ ○ ○ ● ○ ○ ○ ○ ○ ○ ○ ○ ● ○ ○ ○ ○ ○ ○

Worship Christ as Lord of your life. And if someone asks about your hope as a believer, always be ready to explain it. 1 PETER 3:15

66

Q. WHAT IS "BACKSLIDING"?

Is a Christian who backslides still saved?

A. "Backsliding" is the term used for a follower of Jesus who moves away from God instead of growing closer to him. It is not merely sinning. All Christians still sin, even those who are actively trying to serve God. But when a person's heart continually turns away from God and stops trying to obey him, that person is backsliding.

Are backsliding Christians still saved? The real question is whether they ever truly accepted Jesus in the first place. If not, they still have the option to repent and turn to the Lord. Some people who *are* saved go through periods when they get "stuck" in sin or doubt. But God sees our hearts. He knows when life's troubles become too much for us and we fall away. He doesn't want any of his children to be lost, and eventually they will be brought back into fellowship with God. The Holy Spirit will seek them out—and rejoice when they finally return.

○ ○ ○ ○ ○ ○ ○ ○ ○ ○ ○ ● ● ● ● ● ○ ● ○ ○ ○ ○ ○ ○ ○ ○ ● ○ ○ ● ○ ○ ● ○○

There is more joy in heaven over one lost sinner who repents and returns to God than over ninety-nine others who are righteous and haven't strayed away! LUKE 15:7

MORNING BY MORNING, NEW MERCIES I SEE.

FROM THE HYMN
"GREAT IS THY FAITHFULNESS"

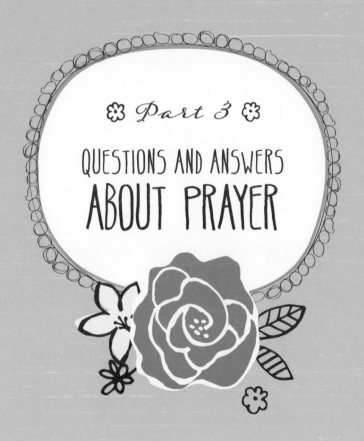

❁ *Part 3* ❁

QUESTIONS AND ANSWERS ABOUT PRAYER

Q. WHAT EXACTLY IS "PRAYER"?

Is it a formal ritual that is only practiced at church or with other people?

A. The most basic explanation of prayer is that it is conversation with God. Prayer is how you communicate with him. You don't have to be in church or with other people to pray. At any moment, you can tell him your thoughts and feelings, express your worries and fears, and ask for his help and guidance. Prayer is also a way to express praise and thankfulness to God for all he does for you. It gives you the opportunity to intercede for others by asking God to heal, strengthen, and help those who need his love and care. Prayer is what puts the "personal" in a personal relationship with God.

God instructs us to pray. He wants us to talk with him. Conversation with God should be even more intimate than conversation with your closest friend or your spouse. You can tell him anything because he wants to know.

Don't worry about anything; instead, pray about everything. Tell God what you need, and thank him for all he has done. Then you will experience God's peace, which exceeds anything we can understand. His peace will guard your hearts and minds as you live in Christ Jesus. PHILIPPIANS 4:6-7

Q. DOES GOD NEED US TO PRAY?

What's in it for him?

A. No, God doesn't need us to pray. God doesn't *need* anything from us. But he does *want* us to pray. In fact, God is so eager for us to pray that he actually commands us to do it. His prayer commands include praying for our enemies (Matthew 5:44) and praying to confess sin (2 Chronicles 7:14). The Bible also instructs us to ask God for wisdom (James 1:5), to pray with "an alert mind and a thankful heart" (Colossians 4:2), and to pray for people in authority (1 Timothy 2:2).

The only way to accurately say that God *needs* us to pray would be to say that he desires a relationship with each of us. God could easily accomplish his work in the world without our help, but instead he chooses to partner with us. Even more than that, he wants to know us, and he wants us to know him. Such a close relationship requires two-way communication: God speaks to us through his Word and through his Spirit in our hearts. We speak to him through prayer—and he listens.

Pray . . . for kings and all who are in authority so that we can live peaceful and quiet lives marked by godliness and dignity. This is good and pleases God our Savior. 1 TIMOTHY 2:2-3

Q. IS THERE SUCH A THING AS TOO MUCH PRAYER?

Doesn't God get tired of hearing from me?

A. Here are just a few reasons God wants you to talk with him:

- God loves you and desires to spend time with you. He wants to know what you're thinking about and how you're feeling.

- When you confess your sins and tell God you're sorry, you can get rid of the guilt that puts a barrier between you.

- God loves it when you praise and honor him and tell him how important he is to you.

- As you feel enough concern to lift another person's needs to God, a bridge is built between you and that person. You are invested in their well-being. God wants his children to love one another that way.

- Prayer, combined with Scripture reading, is a way to seek God's guidance and direction in your life.

    Prayer is one of the greatest privileges and blessings of knowing God. He listens and he answers. And no, God never gets tired of hearing from you.

- -

Come close to God, and God will come close to you.

JAMES 4:8

Q. CAN ANYONE PRAY—EVEN PEOPLE WHO AREN'T CHRISTIANS?

Does God hear and answer their prayers?

A. God knows everything, which means that he *can* hear the prayers of anyone who seeks after him with a sincere heart. And there are instances in Scripture where God answered such prayers. For example, Cornelius was a man who believed in God and prayed regularly, but he didn't yet know about Jesus. God answered his prayers by sending the apostle Peter to tell Cornelius about eternal life through Jesus' sacrifice on the cross. Cornelius believed and was saved! (Acts 10)

God can hear and answer any prayer he chooses. The key to God hearing and answering prayer is to pray "in his will"—with a heart that values the things God values. If you're unsure what God's will is, spend time in his Word, get to know him through prayer, and allow his Spirit to change your heart to be more like him.

God promises to hear and answer the prayers of believers. He also promises to hear and answer the prayers of those who come to him for salvation and are pursuing those things that are in accordance with his will.

- -

The LORD is close to all who call on him, yes, to all who call on him in truth. PSALM 145:18

Q. CAN GOD HEAR EVERYONE'S PRAYERS AT THE SAME TIME?

Wouldn't that get really confusing?

A. We humans move and function within the limits of time, space, physics, and biology. But God doesn't. He has no limits. He is omnipresent, which means that he is present everywhere in the world at the same time. So he can hear your prayer at the very moment millions of others all around the world are praying. He knows everything, sees everything, and hears everything. There are no secrets kept from him.

If God wasn't present everywhere, then he wouldn't be God. His willingness and ability to care for all people at the exact same moment confirms both his limitless nature and his love for every one of his children.

I can never escape from your Spirit! I can never get away from your presence! If I go up to heaven, you are there; if I go down to the grave, you are there. If I ride the wings of the morning, if I dwell by the farthest oceans, even there your hand will guide me, and your strength will me. PSALM 139:7-10

Q. WHAT IS THE PRAYER OF SALVATION?

Where do I find this prayer in the Bible?

A. There is no specific "prayer of salvation" in the Bible. Salvation comes only through faith in Jesus , not through special words spoken. It is offered to you as a free gift based on Jesus' sacrificial death for your sins and his resurrection back to life. Believing in that gift, confessing your sin, and accepting Jesus' forgiveness is what brings salvation.

Prayer can certainly be a way of expressing your faith and verbalizing your acceptance of Jesus, but there are no set words you have to speak or prescribed prayers you must say.

You may often hear ministers suggest that people repeat a prayer after them in order to accept Jesus. That's fine. They are just trying to make things easier. But there is nothing special about the specific words they suggest.

Communicating with God through prayer, confessing your sins, and asking for his help to grow in faith will guide you toward a stronger relationship with him.

Everyone who calls on the name of the LORD will be saved. ROMANS 10:13

73

Q. WHAT IS THE PROPER WAY TO PRAY?

Do I have to kneel and close my eyes for God to listen to my prayer?

A. Yes, there is a right way to pray, but it has nothing to do with whether you are standing or kneeling, eyes closed or open. The proper way to pray is to pray with all your heart—and you can do that no matter your position or location. You can pray while you're driving with eyes wide open. You can whisper a prayer before going into a meeting, or you can carry on a conversation with God while you're working out at the gym. It doesn't matter where you are. It only matters that you trust God and want to connect with him.

Many people do find that prayer comes easier for them in certain postures or situations. Some find that kneeling and closing their eyes helps them focus. Others find that the rhythm of running or walking frees their mind and spirit to pray. Some people find it helpful to write out their prayers. Whatever works for you is the right way to pray.

When you pray, don't babble on and on.... For your Father knows exactly what you need even before you ask him! MATTHEW 6:7-8

74

Q. HOW CAN I TALK TO SOMEONE I CANNOT SEE OR HEAR?

Sometimes it feels like my prayers bounce off the ceiling. Is there a right way to do this?

A. Some people find it hard to pray because they can't see God's face or hear his physical voice. When you're talking with a friend and you can see or hear that person, you know you're connecting. But God is Spirit. How do you communicate with Spirit?

Here are a couple of suggestions to try. If there is a scene or a place in nature where you tend to feel especially close to God, picture that scene when you're praying. Or try concentrating on the image that comes to mind when you think of God—perhaps an artist's image of Jesus. It might help to meditate on a particularly meaningful Bible verse before you start praying or to think about how much God loves you and all the ways he shows that love.

Find the way that makes you feel most connected with God and practice it when you pray. You'll find that the more time you spend in prayer, the more comfortable you'll become.

° ° ° ◦ ° ◦ ◦ ◦ ◦ ° ° ◦ ° ◦ ◦ ◦ ◦ ° ◦ ◦ ◦ ° ° ° ◦ ◦

God is Spirit, so those who worship him must worship in spirit and in truth. JOHN 4:24

Q. WHEN SHOULD I PRAY?

Is it best to have a set time, like in the morning, to pray?

A. The best time to pray is . . . anytime and all the time! There is even a Bible verse that says to "never stop praying" (1 Thessalonians 5:17)—in other words, keep your heart in an attitude of prayer all the time. When you feel a burst of joy, thank God. When you are anxious, call on God for help. When you're afraid, cry out for protection. You get the idea. Know that God is always present with you, always listening, and he wants to hear your prayers.

Many people do find it helpful to set aside a particular time and place in their home for daily prayer and Scripture reading. Others let certain daily experiences—like a morning or evening commute—serve as prayer cues. Some even keep a prayer notebook in which they write down things they want to pray about and answers they've had to their prayers. But know that at any time, whatever you're doing, you can and should talk to your Father who loves you very much!

Pray in the Spirit at all times and on every occasion. Stay alert and be persistent in your prayers for all believers everywhere. EPHESIANS 6:18

Q. WHAT SHOULD I INCLUDE IN MY PRAYERS?

Is there a correct format for prayer?

A. Jesus gave us a format for prayer. It is known as the Lord's Prayer and can be found in Matthew 6:9-13 and Luke 11:2-4. This prayer is not to take the place of your own personal prayers, but it does give a good example of things to include in your conversations with God. It is also a good prayer to pray with other Christians or to recite when you are weary and upset and can't come up with your own words.

The Lord's Prayer emphasizes praising God for who he is and honoring his name and Kingdom. It helps us submit to God's will and trust him to guide and care for us. We tell him what we need and, yes, what we want. We confess our sins and shortcomings and ask for his forgiveness. We ask for his protection in the face of temptation. And we thank him for his faithful answers to our prayers!

Our Father in heaven, may your name be kept holy. May your Kingdom come soon. May your will be done on earth, as it is in heaven. Give us today the food we need, and forgive us our sins, as we have forgiven those who sin against us. And don't let us yield to temptation, but rescue us from the evil one. MATTHEW 6:9-13

Q. TO WHOM DO I PRAY—GOD, JESUS, OR THE HOLY SPIRIT?

Do I have to specify whom I'm talking to, or do they all hear my prayers?

A. You can pray to any or all of the members of the Trinity. They are all God, and they all hear your prayers. Prayers in Scripture are often directed to God the Father. But in the book of Acts when Stephen was about to be stoned to death for his faith, he prayed for Jesus to receive his spirit. And Scripture tells us that the Holy Spirit helps us pray when we cannot find the words ourselves. So all three members of the Trinity are involved in our prayer lives.

With that said, we are not to pray to any other god or person than the triune God. Our loving and caring God does not want us to be swayed by idols or things of this world and desires that we give him all of our worship, praise, and prayers.

● ◦ ◦ ◦   ◦ ◦ ◦ ◦ ◦ ● ◦   ● ◦ ◦ ◦ ◦ ◦ ◦ ● ◦ ◦   ● ◦   ◦ ◦ ◦ ◦ ●

Whatever you do or say, do it as a representative of the Lord Jesus, giving thanks through him to God the Father. COLOSSIANS 3:17

Q. WHY DO PEOPLE PRAY "IN JESUS' NAME"?

Is our prayer not heard if we forget to say those words?

A. It's very common for Christians to finish prayers with the words "in Jesus' name." Jesus actually told us to do that. He said we could ask for anything in his name, and he would grant that request.

To be clear, "anything" means anything that is in God's will. When we pray in Jesus' name, his authority is called on to be the power behind the prayer, so we should be careful what we pray for. Our prayers should be out of concern for ourselves and others and reflect a desire for God's work to be done in the world.

But what if you *don't* end your prayer with "in Jesus' name"? Your prayer will still be heard. This phrase isn't some kind of secret password—it's just a reminder of who makes it possible for us to pray to the Father. Once you have accepted Jesus as your Lord, all your prayers will be in his name—with or without speaking the words.

∘ ⊙ ∘ ⊙ ∘ ∘ ∘ ⊙ ∘ ∘ ∘ ⊙ ∘ ∘ ∘ ∘ ⊙ ⊙ ∘ ∘ ∘ ⊙ ∘ ∘

You can ask for anything in my name, and I will do it, so that the Son can bring glory to the Father. Yes, ask me for anything in my name, and I will do it! JOHN 14:13-14

Q. IS FORMAL LANGUAGE NECESSARY WHEN PRAYING?

Does God only hear my prayers when I use fancy words and phrases?

A. There is no formula to prayer. God does not listen more intently if you use four-syllable words or seventeenth-century English. He doesn't hear you better if you pray Scripture verses back to him. He hears your prayers when they are the sincere cry of your heart. Your prayers should be honest and God honoring. It doesn't matter if you utter only simple words; when those words come from your heart and are directed to God in trust and love, you can be assured that God hears them.

Scripture warns against praying to impress other people. Remember that your prayers, even if delivered in public, are between you and God. Anyone else who is listening may be blessed by your words, but trying to show off is a waste of time. Along the same lines, trying to "preach" or give a message to others through words that are supposedly directed to God is really fulfilling your own desires—not God's.

Pray from your heart in Jesus' name, and believe that God will answer.

- -

When you pray, don't be like the hypocrites who love to pray publicly on street corners and in the synagogues where everyone can see them. I tell you the truth, that is all the reward they will ever get. MATTHEW 6:5

80

Q. COULD SOMETHING BE BLOCKING MY PRAYERS?

Sometimes God and I just aren't connecting. What's wrong?

A. God loves you and wants to be in communication with you. If your prayers don't seem to be getting through, consider these possibilities:

- Maybe there is sin in your life that you're ignoring—pretending that if you don't see it, God doesn't either. Just as a short in an electrical cord prevents connection to a power source, sin can "short out" prayer. Confessing your sin restores the connection and clears the way for good communication with God.

- Perhaps you're determined to do things your way and aren't open to seeking God's will. If so, don't bother asking him to bless your decisions, actions, or choices.

- If you're unwilling to forgive another person, Scripture says that you can't expect God to forgive you.

It's also important to realize that sometimes God wants to grow our faith beyond our feelings. So be assured that if you approach God with the right attitude and spirit, he gladly hears all of your prayers—even if it seems like he doesn't.

- -

When you ask, you don't get it because your motives are all wrong—you want only what will give you pleasure. JAMES 4:3

Q. HOW DO I KNOW WHEN A SITUATION IS AN ANSWER TO PRAYER?

Could what happened be just a coincidence?

A. Faith plays a strong role in the answer to this question—faith that God hears prayers and faith that he answers those that are offered in accordance with his will. When you truly believe this, you can begin watching for his answers and giving him credit for them. There really are no coincidences. God is in control of all things. So if you pray for something and it happens, you can safely assume that God has done what you asked.

Remember, though, that prayer is not like ordering in a restaurant. We don't just put in our orders and wait for God to do what we told him to. God sees a bigger picture than we do, and he answers prayers according to what will be best for us and for his purposes. But God also delights in giving us good things, so don't be surprised if God's answer to your prayer is something far better than you ever imagined.

All glory to God, who is able, through his mighty power at work within us, to accomplish infinitely more than we might ask or think. EPHESIANS 3:20

Q. DIDN'T JESUS SAY I WILL GET WHATEVER I ASK FOR?

I don't see that happening in my life! Am I not praying the right way?

A. Yes, Jesus said we can ask for whatever we want and that God will provide it for us. But that invitation came with a condition: "if you remain in me and my words remain in you" (John 15:7). Otherwise, God would be like Santa Claus or a genie in a magic lamp. You would simply turn in your wish list or rub the lamp and get what you want. But that's not how a relationship with God works. We must be careful to stay close to God, keep reading his Word, and pray for things that honor him and others.

The Bible says we should pray according to God's will, so if you give God a list of selfish or inappropriate requests, you should not expect to receive what you ask for. The same goes if you ask for things that would be bad for you or hurt someone else. Even if you do ask for something that is honoring to God, he may have reasons for not providing it or asking you to wait.

If you remain in me and my words remain in you, you may ask for anything you want, and it will be granted! JOHN 15:7

Q. HOW CAN I BE SURE I AM PRAYING ACCORDING TO GOD'S WILL?

I want to honor God by praying for what he wants, but how can I know what that is?

A. The simple answer is that to pray according to God's will, we must stay close to God. But actually doing that is a learned process. The Bible gives some specific instructions for what to pray about, so it's important to spend time in Scripture. It's also important to pray with an attitude of serving God and others and not with self-serving goals. We must be careful to confess our sins before we come to God with prayer requests and also to remember to thank God for all he does.

Scripture promises that God will give us wisdom if we ask for it, so we should ask him to guide our prayers with his wisdom. Even if we simply do not know what to pray, we can wait in God's presence, and the Holy Spirit will help us.

◦ ◦

The Father who knows all hearts knows what the Spirit is saying, for the Spirit pleads for us believers in harmony with God's own will. ROMANS 8:27

Q. WHAT DO I DO IF THERE DOESN'T SEEM TO BE AN ANSWER TO MY PRAYERS?

I did my best to pray according to God's will. Why doesn't anything seem to be happening?

A. Sometimes God's answer to a prayer is simply no. He knows more than we do and has decided what we asked for isn't best for us.

Other times, God knows it is best for us to practice faith in him and wait for an answer. In the process, our faith and dependence on him will grow, and we'll end up trusting him with whatever the outcome might be.

It's always possible, of course, that we simply missed God's answer. So whenever it seems that God hasn't answered a prayer, it's wise to pay extra attention. What is God trying to tell you? What does he want you to learn?

I will answer them before they even call to me. While they are still talking about their needs, I will go ahead and answer their prayers! ISAIAH 65:24

Q. IF GOD KNOWS EVERYTHING, WHY DO I NEED TO PRAY?

Doesn't he already know what's on my heart?

A. Remember that human beings were created for fellowship with God. Just as we desire to communicate with those we love, God desires for us to be in conversation and relationship with him. Even though God knows our thoughts, he still wants us to express them because doing so will draw us closer to him. So in some ways, prayer is more for us than it is for God.

Praying should be second nature to believers. Our first desire should always be to commune with God—to tell him what we're thinking and feeling and ask for his help and strength. Prayer should involve listening, too—quietly waiting in his presence for him to "speak" (most often through Scripture but also through thoughts or impressions). The more time we spend in prayer, the more we'll recognize God's voice. And as communication with him improves, we'll become more and more aligned with his will, wanting what he wants for us and for the world around us.

Devote yourselves to prayer with an alert mind and a thankful heart. COLOSSIANS 4:2

Q. IS IT OKAY TO PRAY FOR THE SAME THING OVER AND OVER?

Isn't that kind of like nagging God?

A. Yes, it is okay to pray for the same thing over and over. Scripture gives some solid examples of that. One comes from Jesus himself. Before he was arrested, he prayed repeatedly to be spared the suffering he knew was in store (Matthew 26:39-44). Even though God's answer was no and Jesus accepted that, he still felt confident in bringing his concerns to his Father multiple times.

Jesus also told his followers some parables about people who brought their concerns to others time and again. One is about a woman who came to a judge over and over seeking justice for a wrong that had been done to her (Luke 18:1-7). Another tells the story of a man who repeatedly asked a friend for help (Luke 11:5-13). The message behind both of these stories is that it's all right to keep coming to God with our needs and concerns. He does not view it as nagging. Coming to him is what God wants us to do—sharing our hearts and our lives with him.

Keep on asking, and you will receive what you ask for. Keep on seeking, and you will find. Keep on knocking, and the door will be opened to you. MATTHEW 7:7

Q. DO I HAVE TO PRAY OUT LOUD?

Or does God hear my silent prayers?

A. God knows your thoughts, so he knows what's in your heart. That means you don't have to speak your prayers out loud for him to hear you.

There are times when praying silently is best because of the situation you are in—for example, asking for God's help right before you stand up to make a presentation to a large group or praying for wisdom to help a friend who is standing beside you but wouldn't take kindly to your prayer.

Jesus tells us to go somewhere private to pray—to keep our prayers just between ourselves and God. That's another indication that it's fine to pray quietly or silently. On the other hand, if praying out loud helps you concentrate, that's fine too. God hears both your spoken and unspoken prayers. He even hears the prayers that roll quickly through your mind and heart in the midst of your busy days.

You know everything I do. You know what I am going to say even before I say it, LORD. PSALM 139:3-4

Q. IS IT REALLY POSSIBLE TO PRAY ALL THE TIME?

I've heard that the Bible says we should "pray without ceasing."
How do I do this?

A. In his first letter to the church in Thessalonica, the apostle Paul urges his fellow Christians to "never stop praying." A translation that is more familiar to many people is "pray without ceasing" (1 Thessalonians 5:17, KJV). But does that seem impractical or even impossible? When you're working, shouldn't your focus be on what you're doing instead of on praying? How can you carry on a conversation with another person if you are also praying?

Praying without ceasing is possible because it is a heart attitude. It is being continuously submitted to God and connected to him, remaining aware that he is part of every moment of your life. When you have that awareness, you will immediately turn to God whenever worry or fear creeps into your heart. Asking for his help and strength will be an automatic response.

Praying without ceasing is nothing more than full-time trust and dependence on God. Admittedly, this does not come easily, but it is something to practice and to work toward.

○ ○

Always be joyful. Never stop praying. Be thankful in all
circumstances, for this is God's will for you who belong to
Christ Jesus. 1 THESSALONIANS 5:16-18

89

Q. WHAT BENEFIT COMES FROM PRAYING WITH OTHERS?

Does God pay more attention to group prayer than to personal prayer?

A. The major benefit of praying with others is the unity it creates between Christians. When we pray together, we hear that everyone has similar concerns, and that binds us together more closely. As we hear others pray, we learn different ways to bring things before the Lord. And when we hear others pray for us, a sense of belonging and the knowledge that we are cared for grows in our hearts. It's good to know we aren't alone on the journey.

One thing to remember when praying in a group is that your prayers are still just between you and God. Jesus warned against speaking elaborate words just to impress others who are listening to your prayers. Don't try to show off, and try not to be intimidated by the prayers of others.

Group prayers are not more effective in moving God to work than your private prayers. However, the experience of praying with other believers builds community and encourages you to persevere in faith-driven prayer.

- -

Let us think of ways to motivate one another to acts of love and good works. HEBREWS 10:24

Q. HOW DO I PRAY WHEN IT'S HARD TO FORGIVE?

Do I really have to forgive? What if someone hurt me badly?

A. There's a reason God commands us to forgive those who hurt us. Unforgiveness actually hurts us more than it does the other person. It hurts us emotionally by keeping us hung up on the past. It hurts us spiritually because we are refusing to give to another person what God has freely poured out on us, and that creates a barrier between us and God. Unforgiveness can even make us physically ill. That's why God wants us to forgive and move on.

Still, let's be honest—sometimes forgiving is really, really hard. It can even seem impossible. But God can help. Start by confessing that you can't forgive. Ask God to fill you with his grace so that forgiveness can flow from your heart to the other person. You might need to pray that way again and again before you start to feel a change. But through God's power you can eventually experience healing and forgiveness— even if the other person is not at all sorry. Then you will be free, and your prayer life will once again be effective.

- -

Make allowance for each other's faults, and forgive anyone who offends you. Remember, the Lord forgave you, so you must forgive others. COLOSSIANS 3:13

Q. CAN PRAYER CHANGE GOD'S MIND?

Do my prayers have so much effect that they can change God's mind about something?

A. This question has been debated for centuries. There are certainly stories in Scripture of situations where it appears that God changed his actions in response to the prayer requests of his people. In Exodus 32, for instance, Moses talked God out of destroying the Israelites for disobeying him. But does that still happen today?

Since God knows everything that is going to happen, it's hard to say for sure whether our prayers actually change God's mind or the outcome of a situation. When we pray according to his will, we may simply be asking God to do what he has already planned.

On the other hand, God tells us that prayer is powerful, and he promises to listen and respond to our prayers. That would seem to indicate that our prayers can actually affect God's actions in the world as well as help us draw close to him.

Does this mean that every one of our prayers will produce the outcome we're asking for? Most likely not. But if we pray, believing that our prayers are powerful and that God listens, we never know what they can accomplish!

The earnest prayer of a righteous person has great power and produces wonderful results.   JAMES 5:16

Q. WHAT IF OTHERS ARE PRAYING FOR A DIFFERENT OUTCOME FOR THE SAME ISSUE I'M PRAYING ABOUT?

Which one of us will God listen to?

A. Believers on different sides of an issue pray in good faith and with good intentions—for opposing outcomes. So which prayer will God answer?

God's answer has nothing to do with which person he "likes" better. Remember that God sees a bigger picture than humans. He sees the future. He sees other issues and relationships. He sees choices and decisions that will be made down the road.

God's goal in answering any prayer is to move forward his plan for the lives of his children and to accomplish his work on earth. He wants all people to have an opportunity to hear of his love and choose to know him, and he wants his children to live in love with him and one another. So God will respond to competing prayers by giving the answer that best fulfills his purpose.

That's why it's important to remain humble whenever we pray, remembering that nobody but God has all the right answers. Only by remaining close to him can we move closer to the truth.

You can make many plans, but the LORD's purpose will prevail. PROVERBS 19:21

Q. IS IT ALL RIGHT TO PRAY FOR WHAT I WANT?

Will God think I'm selfish?

A. It's perfectly all right to pray for what we want. God wants us to share what we're thinking and feeling, and that includes our desires. Besides, he knows what we're thinking anyway!

At the same time, it's important not to treat God as if he were Santa Claus—just there to give us whatever we want. As a loving parent strives to give us the desires of our hearts, so does our heavenly Father. But God also wants our obedience and our cooperation in accomplishing his work. His answers to our prayers will not contradict his greater purposes.

So yes, pray for your desires. But before you say that prayer, take a moment and consciously submit your heart to God. The closer you stay to him, the more in line your desires will be with his. After you have prayed, pay attention to God's answers. You may get exactly what you asked for. Or you may get something even better as your heavenly Father develops you into the person he wants you to be.

If you sinful people know how to give good gifts to your children, how much more will your heavenly Father give good gifts to those who ask him. MATTHEW 7:11

Q. CAN I PRAY WHEN I KNOW I AM DOING THINGS THAT ARE WRONG?

Will God hear my prayer when I'm caught up in my sin?

A. Sin is rebellion against God. If you choose to continue rebelling but still bring requests to him, you are disregarding—or do not understand—the seriousness of your sin. Scripture tells us that when we continue living in a way that is disobedient to God and does not bring him honor, he gives us up to our sinful desires, severing our relationship with him.

The best prayer to pray when you have been doing things you know are wrong is a prayer of confession and repentance. Through his grace, God will hear your prayer and forgive you. God wants his relationship with you to be unhindered. He wants to hear and answer your prayers. So confess, repent, accept his forgiveness, and ask for his help to refrain from sin. God is for you—not against you—so trust his forgiveness and his ability to help you move forward.

○ ○ ○ ○ ○ ○ ○ ○ ● ○ ● ○ ○ ● ○ ○ ○ ○ ○ ● ○ ○ ● ○ ○ ○ ● ○

Anyone who continues to live in him will not sin. But anyone who keeps on sinning does not know him or understand who he is. 1 JOHN 3:6

Q. WHAT IF I DON'T FEEL LIKE PRAYING?

Sometimes I'm tired and grumpy, and I don't know what to say to God. Can I just skip praying?

A. God doesn't keep score and give demerits every time you choose not to pray. At the same time, consider *why* you don't feel like praying. Are you emotionally exhausted or confused about what to say? Do you doubt that prayer does any good? Every believer experiences this at times. It doesn't make us bad Christians—it just means that we are human beings. Sometimes life beats us down, and our prayer lives can suffer as a result.

The best thing to do when you don't feel like praying is to pray about it! Remind yourself that you can trust God and his Word. Tell God honestly how you feel; then just forge ahead. Keep praying even when you don't feel like it, even if it feels like your prayers hit the ceiling and bounce back. Keep telling God what's on your heart, and ask him to increase your faith. If you can't find the words, consider praying passages from Scripture (especially the Psalms) or a good devotional book. Keep doing what you know you should be doing, and this season of dryness will eventually pass.

Jesus said, "Come to me, all of you who are weary and carry heavy burdens, and I will give you rest." MATTHEW 11:28

Q. WHAT IF I JUST . . . CAN'T PRAY?

What do I do when I'm too overwhelmed to pray?

A. Some situations are so intense, frightening, or painful that we simply don't know how to pray. We don't know what to ask God for, what words we should say, or even how he could make the situation better. What do we do then?

Remember that God's Holy Spirit is living in your heart. When you don't know what to pray, ask him to pray for you. God promises to do that. He knows there will be times when you are at a loss for words and all you can do is lean on him for strength.

Don't forget to lean on other believers as well. Ask for their prayers, and accept their spiritual—and physical—support. The Bible commands us to "share each other's burdens" (Galatians 6:2), and this means accepting help as well as giving it.

Remember that God loves you very much, and he will not abandon you in times of need. You can trust him to hear and answer you even when you're too overwhelmed to ask.

The Holy Spirit helps us in our weakness. . . . The Holy Spirit prays for us with groanings that cannot be expressed in words. ROMANS 8:26

Q. WHAT IS "INTERCESSORY PRAYER"?

Am I supposed to do it?

A. Intercessory prayer is simply prayer on behalf of other people and specific situations. It is modeled often in Scripture by people like Moses, King David, Elijah, and Daniel. Jesus himself prayed often for others, especially for his disciples.

An intercessor comes to God humbly, believing God will answer and that he deeply loves the person being prayed for and cares about the circumstances that are at stake. The intercessor prays fervently and persistently for God's best for the person or situation and accepts God's answer as the best one.

Anyone can pray in this way. When God puts someone's name or a situation on your heart, you should certainly go to the Lord with a heart to intercede. You can also keep a list of people whom you want to pray for, and you can ask others to pray for you. The process of intercession brings people together for a common cause and grows your relationship with other believers. Many people who are the focus of such prayer claim they can "feel" the spiritual support.

I urge you, first of all, to pray for all people. Ask God to help them; intercede on their behalf, and give thanks for them. 1 TIMOTHY 2:1

Q. WHAT ARE SOME DIFFERENT WAYS TO PRAY?

Isn't all prayer just prayer?

A. Yes, prayer is prayer. But just as there are different ways for human beings to communicate with one another, there are different approaches to prayer. If one type of prayer doesn't seem to be effective in a certain circumstance, trying a different approach can often help. Here are a few possibilities:

- *Conversational prayer*—talking to God in everyday language— is the most accessible kind of prayer for most people.

- *Meditation* is an ancient Christian practice that stresses remaining quiet and attentive, listening for God's voice.

- *Praying Scripture* is often done with the Psalms—simply reading a passage silently or aloud as a prayer. It's helpful when we're not sure what to pray.

- *Group prayer* brings unity and power to gatherings of believers.

- *Journaled prayer* is written prayer. Many people find this helps them understand what they are praying, and they enjoy being able to look back on prayers over time.

Seek his will in all you do, and he will show you which path to take. PROVERBS 3:6

Q. WHAT DOES IT MEAN TO "PUT OUT A FLEECE"?

Do I need to do that?

A. "Putting out a fleece" means asking God to prove that it's his voice you're hearing. It comes from the story of Gideon (Judges, chapter 6). The angel of the LORD told Gideon he would rescue Israel from invaders who were stealing their crops. But Gideon was unwilling to move forward until he was convinced it was God's plan. So Gideon laid a fleece on the ground and asked God to make the wool wet with dew the next morning—while keeping the ground dry. God, in his grace, did it. Then Gideon asked that the next morning he would find the fleece dry and the ground wet. Once again, God did it.

It isn't necessary for believers today to put out a fleece so God can prove himself. God's Holy Spirit lives in their hearts, prompting them with guidance to know God's will. We also have the Bible, which helps us understand God more completely. Gideon's story is a good example of the importance of knowing God's leading, but God need not prove himself to us. We can just talk to God and trust him. Even if we mistake his leading, God can still work things out.

- -

God causes everything to work together for the good of those who love God and are called according to his purpose. ROMANS 8:28

Q. DOES FASTING MAKE PRAYER MORE EFFECTIVE?

How so, and how do you do it?

A. Fasting means you decide to abstain from eating or some other regular activity for a specified length of time. Fasting can free you from daily concerns or compulsions and help you focus attention and energy on an issue that is weighing on your heart. It can also help you realize how much you need God and prioritize your relationship with him over other areas of life.

Both the Old and New Testaments give examples of God's people devoting themselves to prayer and fasting, especially when faced with serious issues. They found it to be a powerful way to draw closer to the Lord. Fasting can serve the same purpose today. It's a weapon you have been given to make your communication with God more intimate and impactful.

It's probably best to start with a short fast and work up from there. If you're unsure about how to fast safely, you can find helpful tips in Christian books and on the Internet. People with certain medical conditions should *not* fast, so it's wise to first consult with your physician.

Everything else is worthless when compared with the infinite value of knowing Christ Jesus my Lord. For his sake I have discarded everything else, counting it all as garbage, so that I could gain Christ. PHILIPPIANS 3:8

Q. WHY DO PEOPLE PUT SO MUCH EMPHASIS ON THANKING GOD IN THEIR PRAYERS?

Does hearing my thanks really make a difference to God?

A. Most children are taught to say thank you for any gift or kindness shown to them. God desires that same kind of training for his children.

There are several commands in the Bible reminding us to thank God for all he does and all he gives to us. Why? Because each time we stop and thank God, we are reminded that all we have—all we are—is a gift from him. He is the source of everything—from our creation and salvation to the food we eat and the air we breathe. That simple "thank you" before a meal, in daily prayers, or even in a random moment when we feel gratitude reinforces our sense of dependence on God and our recognition of his power, strength, and love.

Giving thanks for beautiful and pleasant things is relatively easy. But the Bible tells us to be thankful even for the things that are difficult or painful. In such times, our dependence on God and our trust in him grows deeper. Difficult times are often times of growth, and that's also a reason for gratitude.

Give thanks to the Lord, for he is good! His faithful love endures forever.   PSALM 106:1